A CONCISE GUIDE TO
EUROPEAN PATENTS:
LAW AND PRACTICE

AUSTRALIA
The Law Book Company
Brisbane • Sydney • Melbourne • Perth

CANADA
Carswell
Ottawa • Toronto • Calgary • Montreal • Vancouver

AGENTS
Steimatzky's Agency Ltd., Tel Aviv
N.M. Tripathi (Private) Ltd., Bombay
Eastern Law House (Private) Ltd., Calcutta
M.P.P. House, Bangalore
Universal Book Traders, Delhi
Aditya Books, Delhi
MacMillan Shuppan KK, Tokyo
Pakistan Law House, Karachi, Lahore

A CONCISE GUIDE TO
EUROPEAN PATENTS:
LAW AND PRACTICE

BY

GERALD PATERSON M.A. (OXON)

Barrister-at-law, Gray's Inn, London;
Chairman of a Technical Board of Appeal,
European Patent Office, Munich

LONDON
SWEET & MAXWELL
1995

Published in 1995 by Sweet & Maxwell Limited of
South Quay Plaza, 183 Marsh Wall, London E14 9FT.
Phototypeset by LBJ Enterprises Ltd. of Aldermaston and Chilcompton.
Printed and bound in Great Britain by Butler and Tanner Ltd., Frome and
London.

No natural forests were destroyed to make this product;
only farmed timber was used and replanted.

A CIP catalogue record for this book is available from the British Library

ISBN 0 421 53550 4

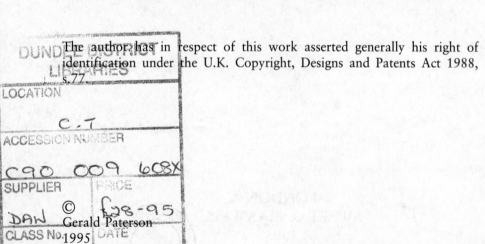

To

HIROKO

and

ALEXANDER, EDWARD, VANESSA

Preface

The European Patent Office opened in 1978, and since then, the European patent system has developed impressively, with generally increasing numbers of European patent applications filed each year. The system is based upon the European Patent Convention, a treaty signed by currently 17 European countries (the "Contracting States"), which provides a centralised system for granting European patents.

The current and future scale of operation of the European Patent Office is such that industry worldwide needs to be aware, through its advisers, of the current state of the procedural and substantive law concerning the grant of European patents. The author's work *The European Patent System* published in English by Sweet & Maxwell, London, in 1992 is intended to meet that need by providing a comprehensive discussion of the jurisprudence which has been developed and which is still developing; but its length may limit its utility, especially for patent attorneys and patent managers who need to understand how the European patent system works and the principles which underlie it, but do not often need a full discussion of its details.

This book is a shorter work containing the essential principles of the procedural and substantive law of the European patent system at its current stage of development.

The first chapter contains an outline of the more important features of the European patent system and the organs which control its development. The remaining chapters are shortened, updated versions of corresponding sections of *The European Patent System*. Chapters two to five describe examination, opposition and appeal procedure at the European Patent Office, and the remaining chapters analyse the substantive jurisprudence concerning the grant of European patents. Any reader who needs more detailed information than provided by this book should therefore consult *The European Patent System*.

As far as possible, decisions of the Boards of Appeal of the European Patent Office which have been published in the Official Journal of the European Patent Office before January 1, 1995 have been taken into account, as well as some decisions which will be so published in the near future.

Views which have been expressed in this book are entirely those of the author.

Gerald Paterson
Munich, Germany
January 27, 1995

Contents

Tables of Cases

A NOTE ON THE IDENTIFICATION OF DECISIONS
Every decision issued by a Board of Appeal is identified by a letter, a number and the year in which it was issued. The different categories of decision issued by the Boards of Appeal with which this book is concerned are identified by letters as follows:

Enlarged Board of Appeal .. G
Legal Board of Appeal ...... J
Technical Boards of Appeal T

Almost every decision issued by a Board of Appeal is also identified by a "headword," consisting of the name of the applicant or patentee, and a short title.

The European Patent Office ("EPO") has adopted the practice of referring to individual decisions generally by number, rather than by headword or name of the applicant or patentee. This practice has been followed in the text of this book.

In order to help the identification of individual decisions referred to in this book, every numbered decision in the text is referred to in a footnote with a reference to its place of publication, if any. Decisions which have not been published either in the Official Journal of the EPO ("O.J. EPO") or in the European Patent Office Reports of the EPO ("EPOR") are accompanied by their date of issue. A decision which is scheduled for publication in the Official Journal but which is not yet so published is additionally marked with a (P).

The Tables of Cases which follow correlate the numbers of the decisions with their headwords. The first Table sets out the decisions in chronological and numerical order, and the second Table sets out the decisions in the alphabetical order of their headwords. A particular decision may therefore be located in the text of the book on the basis either of its number or of its headword.

The Official Journal is published monthly by the European Patent Office. The European Patent Office Reports are published eight times a year in English by Sweet & Maxwell, London.

Table 1: Chronological and Numerical Order

ENLARGED BOARD OF APPEAL CASES

BOARD OF APPEAL CASES — LEGAL BOARD

FIRST INSTANCE DECISION

EUROPEAN NATIONAL CASES

Table 2: Alphabetical Order

ENLARGED BOARD OF APPEAL CASES

BOARD OF APPEAL CASES — LEGAL BOARD

BOARD OF APPEAL CASES — TECHNICAL BOARDS

First Instance Decision

European National Cases

Table of Treaties, Conventions, Rules and Protocols, etc.

Table of Abbrevations

Budapest	Budapest Treaty on the International Recognition of the Deposit of Micro-organisms
COPAC	Common Appeal Court (under CPC)
CPC	Community Patent Convention
EPC	European Patent Convention
EPO	European Patent Office
EPOR	European Patent Office Reports
G	Prefix to EPO Decision numbers indicating Enlarged Board of Appeal Decisions
Guidelines	Guidelines for Examination in the EPO
J	Prefix to EPO Decision numbers indicating Legal Board of Appeal Decisions
O.J. EPO	Official Journal of the EPO
(P)	Used in case citations to indicate that a Decision is due to be published in the O.J. EPO
Paris	Paris Convention for the Protection of Industrial Property
PCT	Patent Co-operation Treaty
RPBA	Rules of Procedure of the Boards of Appeal
RPEBA	Rules of Procedure of the Enlarged Board of Appeal
T	Prefix to EPO Decision numbers indicating Technical Boards of Appeal Decisions
UPOV Convention	International Convention for the Protection of New Varieties of Plants
Vienna	Vienna Convention on the Law of Treaties

1. Outline of the European Patent System

CONTENTS

A. INTRODUCTION

The European patent system is currently primarily concerned with the **1–01** granting of European patents, and therefore with their validity but not with their enforcement. The system is based upon the codification of patent law which came into force in 1978 as the European Patent Convention[1] (the EPC), in coexistence with individual national patent laws. The EPC is the first of two pillars of the European patent system. The second pillar, the Community Patent Convention[2] (the CPC), is also

---

[1] Convention on the Grant of European Patents – signed Munich, 1973.
[2] Convention for the European Patent for the Common Market – signed Luxembourg, 1975, amended Luxembourg, 1985 and 1989.

concerned with the enforcement of European patents by means of infringement proceedings in national courts, and is discussed further in paragraph
1–15 below. The CPC is not yet in force.

The main objects of the EPC, as set out in its preamble, are "to
strengthen co-operation between the States of Europe in respect of the
protection of inventions", and "that such protection may be obtained in
those States by a single procedure for the grant of patents and by the
establishment of certain standard rules governing patents so granted."

Currently, 17 European countries have signed the EPC and are Con-
tracting States: Austria, Belgium, Denmark, France, Germany, Greece,
Ireland, Italy, Liechtenstein, Luxembourg, Monaco, Netherlands, Portugal,
Spain, Sweden, Switzerland and the United Kingdom. The protection
conferred by European patents can also be extended to Lithuania and
Slovenia.[3]

B. IMPORTANT CHARACTERISTICS OF THE EPC

(a) A "first-to-file" system

1–02 The European patent system is a "first-to-file" system, like previous
European national patent systems, and like the Japanese patent system, but
unlike the American patent system, which is a "first-to-invent" system.
According to the European system, therefore, if two or more persons make
the same invention independently of each other, only the person who first
files a European patent application can obtain a European patent.

When a European patent application is filed at the EPO, it receives a
filing date. Patentability having regard to novelty and inventive step is
assessed in relation to the state of the art at the filing date (unless priority
is lawfully claimed from an earlier filed application under the Paris
Convention, in which case the priority date counts as the filing date – see
paragraph 9–01 below). Furthermore, the contents of such a European
patent application become part of the state of the art on its filing date with
respect to a later filed European patent application for the purpose of
assessing its novelty – see paragraphs 10–02 and 10–12 below.

(b) Early publication of a European patent application

1–03 One important aspect of the EPC compared to previous European
national patent laws is the requirement for early publication of a European
patent application, namely, as soon as possible after the expiry of a period
of 18 months from the date of filing, or, if priority has been claimed, from
the date of priority – Article 93 EPC. This requirement serves the
important function of making the information contained in European
patent applications available to the public at an early stage. However,
since a decision as to the grant of a European patent can rarely be made so

---

[3] See O.J. EPO 1994, 75 and 527.

quickly, an applicant is in effect forced to have the subject matter of his application published before he knows whether the application will be successful.

(c) Nature of a European patent: a bundle of national patents

The EPC provides a centralised system for granting European patents 1–04 having effect in one or more of the Contracting States. Upon filing a European patent application at the European Patent Office (the "EPO"), the applicant is required to designate the Contracting States in which protection is desired. Upon grant, a European patent becomes a bundle of national patents having effect in each of such designated Contracting States for a term of 20 years from the date of filing of the application (Article 63(1) EPC). After grant, apart from the centralised opposition procedure before the EPO, which in accordance with Article 99 EPC may be commenced within nine months from grant (see Chapter 3), a European patent is no longer within the competence of the EPO; the resulting bundle of national patents may only be challenged and enforced individually within the national jurisdictions of the designated Contracting States.

C. THE FIRST AND SECOND INSTANCE DEPARTMENTS OF THE EPO

The first instance departments of the EPO whose decisions may be the 1–05 subject of an appeal are the Receiving Section, the Examining Divisions and the Opposition Divisions, which are concerned with examination and opposition; and the Legal Division.

The Receiving Section is in the branch of the EPO at The Hague, and is responsible for the examination on filing and the examination as to formal requirements of each European patent application. A European search report is then drawn up by a Search Division, also based at The Hague.

An Examining Division is thereafter responsible for the substantive examination of each such application, as to whether the application or the invention to which it relates meets the requirements of the EPC, in particular the requirements for patentability, so that a European patent can be granted (see Chapter 2).

Within nine months of grant of a European patent, any person may file an opposition to the granted patent, on one or more grounds which are specified in the EPC. An Opposition Division is responsible for the examination of such an opposition (see Chapter 3).

The Legal Division is responsible for decisions concerning entries in the Register of European Patents, and entries in the list of professional representatives.

The basic practice of the first instance departments of the EPO, which are concerned with examination and opposition, is set out in the *Guidelines for Examination in the EPO*, which are published by and obtainable from the EPO. Such a department can be expected to follow the *Guidelines*, so far as applicable to a particular case. The *Guidelines* are quite frequently amended, *inter alia* in response to changes in the Rules of the EPC and in response to decisions of the Boards of Appeal.

If a party to proceedings before a first instance department is "adversely affected" by a decision of such a department, he may appeal to one of the Boards of Appeal ("the second instance"). Following examination of such an appeal, the Board of Appeal issues reasons for its decision on the appeal in writing (see Chapter 4).

D. The Boards of Appeal: the Second Instance

(a) Introduction

1–06   Article 106 EPC provides an appeal as of right from every decision issued by one of the above first instance departments of the EPO, to a Board of Appeal. The Boards of Appeal are in every case the second and final instance within the EPO. If a European patent application is refused or a European patent is revoked by a decision of a Board of Appeal, no further appeal is possible either within or outside the EPO, and such decision is therefore final in all respects.

At present over a thousand appeals from decisions of first instance departments are filed each year, and about a thousand written decisions are issued by the Boards of Appeal each year. The more important of these decisions of the Boards of Appeal, concerning points of law and interpretation of the EPC, are published in the Official Journal of the EPO ("O.J. EPO"), which is issued monthly. These important decisions, in combination with the practice represented in all the other Boards of Appeal decisions which have been issued, constitute the ultimate authority on practice within the EPO, and form a body of jurisprudence which is central to the European patent system. The substance of this book is therefore based upon such jurisprudence.

(b) Organisation of the Boards of Appeal

1–07   The Boards of Appeal are administratively organised as one of five Directorates-General within the EPO. This is essentially for ease of organisation, however; the Boards of Appeal are intended to operate entirely independently from the first instance departments which make the decisions which are the subject of appeals, and from the administration of the EPO. This independence of operation is guaranteed as far as possible by the independent status of the individual members of the Boards of Appeal, as provided in particular by Article 23 EPC.

The Boards of Appeal act as courts with the task of ensuring that the provisions of the EPC are applied in practice in each individual case.[4]

Member of the Boards of Appeal must be either legally or technically qualified. There are about three times as many technically qualified members as legally qualified members.

---

4 G1/86 O.J. EPO 1987, 447.

The large majority of appeals are from decisions of the Examining Divisions and the Opposition Divisions concerning the grant or maintenance of a European patent, and these are decided by Technical Boards of Appeal.

There are currently four Technical Boards of Appeal for Chemistry, five Technical Boards for Mechanics, two Technical Boards for Electricity, and two Technical Boards for Physics. Individual appeals from the Examining Divisions and the Opposition Divisions are assigned when filed to specific Technical Boards of Appeal in accordance with the international classification of the technical subject matter of the patent application or patent which is the subject of the case.

Each Technical Board of Appeal is composed of a permanent Chairman (who may be either technically or legally qualified) and usually four or five other permanent members. Each individual appeal is normally heard and decided by three members, two technical and one legal member. In appropriate cases, however, a Technical Board may be enlarged to five members, three technical and two legal members, under Article 21(3) and (4) EPC. The Chairman of each Technical Board of Appeal designates the members of his Board who are to be responsible for an individual appeal, when it is filed.

In addition to the Technical Boards of Appeal, there is a Legal Board of Appeal consisting of a permanent Chairman and a number of other members, who are all legally qualified. The Legal Board of Appeal is responsible for deciding all appeals from the Receiving Section and the Legal Division, and appeals from the Examining Divisions which are not concerned with the refusal or grant of a European patent. Each individual appeal is heard and decided by three legal members.

(c) The Enlarged Board of Appeal

The Enlarged Board of Appeal is responsible for deciding important points of law which are referred to it by individual Boards of Appeal or by the President of the EPO under Article 112 EPC. It constitutes the highest judicial authority within the Boards of Appeal, and is composed of five legal members, including its Chairman, and two technical members.   1–08

The mechanism by which points of law are referred to the Enlarged Board of Appeal is discussed in paragraph 4–50.

E. Interpretation of the EPC by the Boards of Appeal

As mentioned in paragraph 1–05 above, the *Guidelines for Examination in the EPO* constitute a basic guide to interpretation of the EPC which the first instance departments of the EPO normally follow. The *Guidelines* do not bind the Boards of Appeal, which act as courts by applying the requirements of the EPC directly to each case before them.   1–09

Individual Boards of Appeal are not bound to follow previous interpretations of the EPC as set out in earlier Board of Appeal decisions, but they usually do, and therefore most provisions of the EPC are already the subject of an established jurisprudence within the Boards of Appeal (and therefore also within the first instance departments of the EPO). In the event of divergent interpretations of the EPC by different Boards of Appeal in different decisions the Enlarged Board of Appeal may be asked to decide on the important point of law in issue – see paragraphs 4–49 to 4–52.

In deciding upon the interpretation of the EPC, the Boards of Appeal (including the Enlarged Board of Appeal) apply the Vienna Convention[5]; Articles 31 to 33 of this Convention contain a clear and relatively short statement as to how an international treaty such as the EPC should be interpreted. In particular, such a treaty must be interpreted in good faith, and its terms must be given their ordinary meaning in their context and in the light of its object and purpose.

Additionally, the Boards of Appeal have applied a number of inter-nationally recognized "general principles of law", when deciding points of law which arise in cases before them. Examples of such general principles of law which have been applied are:

(1) The principle of good faith (between the EPO and parties before it)[6];
(2) Equality of treatment of parties[7];
(3) The right to a fair hearing[8];
(4) The duty to give reasons for decisions.[9]

F. RELATIONSHIP OF THE BOARDS OF APPEAL WITH NATIONAL COURTS: HARMONIZATION

(a) The nature of the harmonization process

1–10   The Contracting States to the EPC are not bound to bring their national patent laws into conformity with the EPC, but since the harmonization of patent law within Europe is the main purpose of the EPC, the majority of such States have changed their national patent laws so that they do so conform. Therefore, many provisions of the EPC, concerning both pro-cedural law and substantive law, have courterparts in individual national patent laws.

In individual cases, the EPO (including the Boards of Appeal) on the one hand and national courts on the other hand may be called upon to decide the same or similar questions of interpretation of the same or similar provisions. Neither the Boards of Appeal nor national courts are legally bound to follow previous decisons or judgments of each other; but having regard to the common background of a desire for harmonization within Europe, previous decisions of the EPO (in particular the Boards of Appeal)

---

[5] Convention on the Law of Treaties – signed Vienna, 1969.
[6] e.g. J10/84 O.J. EPO 1985, 71; J3/87 O.J. EPO 1989, 3; G5, 7 and 8/88 O.J. EPO 1991, 137.
[7] e.g. G1/86 O.J. EPO 1987, 447.
[8] e.g. J20/85 O.J. EPO 1987, 102; G5/91 O.J. EPO 1992, 617.
[9] e.g. T182/88 O.J. EPO 1990, 287.

concerning such points of law which are common to the EPC and national laws are strongly persuasive upon national courts, and vice versa.

The desire for harmonization of patent law within Europe can therefore be considered as an additional factor which may influence the interpretation of the EPC. Since the EPC directly creates and defines the rights and duties of individuals and legal entities, when interpreting such a treaty it is necessary to pay attention to the question of harmonization of national and international rules of law.[10]

(b) Harmonization of substantive patent law: examples

The most important area of substantive patent law in which a consider- 1–11 able degree of harmonization can be seen to have been achieved between the jurisprudence of the Boards of Appeal and that of national courts is that concerning patentability (Articles 52 to 57 EPC).

Thus, the "second medical use" jurisprudence of the Boards of Appeal (see paragraph 10–30 below) has been followed by national courts in the United Kingdom and Sweden, in the interest of achieving conformity under the EPC. The House of Lords in the United Kingdom has followed Boards of Appeal jurisprudence concerning the necessity for an "enabling disclosure" (see paragraph 10–26 below) if a prior published document is to be novelty-destroying. The jurisprudence and practice of the EPO concerning the patentability of micro-organisms and the requirements for reproducibility of such inventions had been followed by the German Federal Court of Justice, for reasons of a desirable uniform interpretation of the law. The jurisprudence of the Boards of Appeal concerning the patentability of methods used in conjunction with computer programs (see paragraphs 8–05 and 8–06 below) has been followed by the Swedish Supreme Administrative Court.

G. Infringement Proceedings before National Courts: the Extent of Protection

(a) Introduction

When a European patent is granted, it has the effect in each designated 1–12 Contracting State of a national patent granted by that State (Articles 2 and 64(1) EPC). It thus becomes a bundle of national patents which are subject to the national laws of the individual designated States (see paragraph 1–04 above). Any alleged infringement of a European patent is dealt with by national law (Article 64(3) EPC).[11]

(b) Role of the claims in determining the extent of protection

The claims of a European patent application are required to define the 1–13 subject matter, in terms of the technical features of the invention, for which protection is sought (Article 84 and Rule 29(1) EPC). The primary

---

[10] G5/83 O.J. EPO 1985, 64.
[11] G4/91 O.J. EPO 1993, 707.

aim of the wording of a claim is therefore to satisfy this requirement, having regard to the nature of the invention.

The purpose of claims under the EPC is to enable the protection conferred by the patent to be determined (Article 69(1) EPC), and thus the rights of the patent proprietor within the designated Contracting States (Articles 64(1) EPC),[12] having regard to the patentability requirements of Articles 52 to 57 EPC.

(c) The interpretation of claims by national courts

1–14   Determination of the extent of protection conferred by a European patent has to be carried out in accordance with Article 69(1) EPC and its Protocol. The main role of the claims is emphasised in the first sentence of Article 69(1) EPC, and the subsidiary role of the description and drawings is set out in the second sentence. The relationship between the claims, and the description and drawings, when determining the extent of protection of a European patent is further explained in the Protocol to Article 69 EPC.

Before the EPC entered into effect, the extent to which the wording of claims determined the scope of protection varied within Europe from country to country. The Protocol to Article 69 EPC was adopted as an integral part of the EPC in order to provide a mechanism for harmonization of the various national approaches to the interpretation of claims, and is primarily directed to providing an intermediate method of interpretation as a compromise between such previous national approaches, with the object of combining "a fair protection" for the patentee with a reasonable degree of certainty for third parties.[13]

Against the above background, inevitably the diferent traditional national approaches to interpretation of claims still exert some influence in national infringement proceedings, with a consequent possibility of different results on the same facts and under the same European patent in different Contracting States.[14]

H. The Community Patent Convention: the Next Stage of the European Patent System

1–15   The next stage of development of the European patent system will be based upon the Community Patent Convention (CPC). The contents of this important treaty have been generally agreed, but the treaty is subject to ratification by the Contracting States, and the timetable for this is uncertain. It is therefore not yet in force.

Under the CPC it will be possible to obtain a Community patent, having a unitary character and equal effect throughout the territories of the European Community (EC).

---

[12] G2/88 O.J. EPO 1990, 93.
[13] *Ibid.*
[14] See paragraphs 11–12 to 11–17 of Paterson, *The European Patent System* (1992).

Of particular significance also is the system of international jurisdiction which is to be set up under the Protocol on Litigation, which is an integral part of the CPC.

Under this Protocol, litigation at first instance concerning Community patents is divided between Revocation Divisions of the EPO and designated national courts, called Community patent courts. The Revocation Divisions will have exclusive jurisdiction concerning proceedings for amendment and revocation of Community patents, and the Community patent courts will have exclusive jurisdiction concerning other proceedings involving infringement and validity of Community patents.

Second instance proceedings concerning appeals from Revocation Divisions and Community patent courts will be heard and decided by a Common Appeal Court, called COPAC. The Common Appeal Court will therefore be ultimately responsible for a continuing harmonization of all aspects of European patent law.

2. Examination Procedure

CONTENTS

A. INTRODUCTION

2–01   The requirements for the substantive contents of a European patent application (*i.e.* the description, claims and drawings) are considered in Chapter 6 below. The substantive requirements for patentability are considered in Chapters 8, 10 and 11 below.

Substantive examination of a patent application by an Examining Division, to ensure its conformity with the requirements in the EPC for grant of a patent, is governed by Article 96 and Rule 51 EPC, and is based upon the contents of the European search report so far as the requirements for novelty (Chapter 10) and inventive step (Chapter 11) are concerned. The European search report is drawn up by a Search Division of the EPO pursuant to Articles 17 and 92 EPC.

An Examining Division consists of three technical examiners, one of which is the primary examiner. An additional legally qualified examiner may also form part of an Examining Division, "if the nature of the decision so requires" (Article 18(2) EPC).

Under Article 18(1) EPC, the Examining Division is responsible for the examination of a European patent application from the time when the Receiving Section ceases to be responsible: that is, upon filing of a request for examination or of an indication under Article 96(1) EPC that the applicant desires to proceed with the application.

The procedure which should be followed by the Examining Divisions is dealt with comprehensively in the *Guidelines* (see para. 1–05 above).

B. Filing a Patent Application

(a) Contents

According to Article 78 EPC a European patent application shall contain: 2–02

(1) a request for a patent:
(2) a description of the invention;
(3) one or more claims;
(4) any drawings referred to in the description or claims;
(5) an abstract.

However, according to Article 80 EPC, in order to be allocated a filing date an application need only contain:

(1) an indication that a patent is sought;
(2) the designation of a least one Contracting State;
(3) information identifying the applicant;
(4) a description and one or more claims.

(b) Place and time of filing

An application may be filed at any one of the filing offices of the EPO in   2–03
Munich, The Hague and Berlin.[1] In addition, Article 75(1)(b) EPC provides that an application may be filed at "the central industrial

---

[1] Article 75(1)(a) EPC, and Decisions of the President of the EPO dated May 10, 1989 and March 18, 1991; O.J. EPO 1989, 218 and O.J. EPO 1991, 223.

11

property office or other competent authority" of a Contracting State, if the law of that State so permits.

The date of filing of an application is the date of receipt of documents making up the application in accordance with Article 80 EPC, either directly at the EPO or at a competent national authority. The date of filing of an application is determined in accordance with Rule 24 EPC, wherever it is filed.[2]

(c) Language

2–04   A patent application must be filed in one of the three official languages of the EPO (English, French and German) — Article 14(1) EPC; this is subject to the provision in Article 14(2) EPC that "natural or legal persons having their residence or principal place of business" within a Contracting State having a language other than English, French or German as an official language may file an application in such official language, provided that a translation into English, French or German is filed within a prescribed period (Rule 6(1) EPC). Such translation may accompany the application.[3]

A 20 per cent reduction in filing and examination fees is provided by Rule 6(3) EPC to an applicant who files an application in such a language. It is sufficient if the description and claims are filed in such a language.[4]

(d) Representation

2–05   Article 134 EPC provides that a person who has either a residence or his principal place of business with a Contracting State need not be represented by a professional representative in any proceedings before the EPO, and thus may file a patent application and prosecute it himself. Such a person may also be represented by an authorised employee (who need not be a professional representative),

However, in accordance with Article 133(2) EPC a person who does not have either a residence or his principal place of business within a Contracting State must be represented by a professional representative and act through him in all proceedings before the EPC. This is subject to the exception that such a person may file a European patent application without such a representative: thereafter a professional representative is required for prosecution of the application.

Evidence may be taken pursuant to Article 117(1)(a) EPC by hearing a party in the absence of a professional representative.[5]

Article 133(2) EPC states that the Rules may provide other exceptions to the requirement for professional representation, but at the time of writing no further exceptions have been made.

---

[2] J18/86 O.J. EPO 1988, 165.
[3] G6/91 O.J. EPO 1992, 491.
[4] J4/88 O.J. EPO 1989, 483.
[5] T451/89 April 1, 1993.

A list of professional representatives is maintained by the EPO pursuant to Article 134(1) EPC. Every such professional representative must be a national of a Contracting State, must have his place of business or employment within a Contracting State, and must have passed the European Qualifying Examination.

(e) Identity of the applicant

Article 80(c) EPC requires *inter alia* that "information identifying the applicant" shall be contained in the application documents, if a date of filing of the application is to be allocated to it.   **2–06**

This requirement is satisfied whenever it is possible to establish the identity of the applicant beyond reasonable doubt on the basis of all data contained in the documents filed.[6]

C. EXAMINATION PROCEDURE

(a) Extent of the examination

The Examining Division is responsible for examining whether a European Patent application meets "the requirements of the EPC" (Articles 94(1) and 96(2) EPC).   **2–07**

Under Article 167(2) EPC, upon joining the EPC a Contracting State may make certain reservations concerning what may be protected by a European patent (*e.g.* certain States have made reservations concerning chemical, pharmaceutical and food products). Such reservations are part of national laws and are not "requirements of the EPC" which have to be considered by the Examining Division when examining an application under Article 96(2) EPC[7]. It is the applicant's responsibility to file appropriate claims having regard to any such reservations.

(b) Communications and observations in reply

(i) The first communication — a right to reply

Article 96(2) EPC requires the Examining Division, when raising one or more grounds of objection to the grant of a patent, to invite the applicant to file observations in reply within a fixed period, normally of between two and four months. Thus, the applicant has a right to reply to the first communication within this fixed period. Furthermore, pursuant to Rule 86(3) EPC the applicant has a right to amend the description, claims or drawings at this stage, provided that the amendments are filed at the same time as the observations in reply.   **2–08**

(ii) Failure to reply in due time

Article 96(3) EPC provides that "If the applicant fails to reply in due time to [an invitation under Article 96(2) EPC], the application shall be deemed to be withdrawn." (This sanction is subject to a request for further processing under Article 121 EPC — see paragraph 5–02, below.)   **2–09**

---

[6] J25/86 O.J. EPO 1987, 475; J21/87, December 21, 1987.
[7] G7/93 O.J. EPO 1994, 775.

(iii) Further communications compared with issue of a decision

2–10   Article 96(2) EPC requires that the Examining Division shall invite the applicant "as often as necessary" to file his observations. This requirement implicitly recognizes that in certain circumstances there is a legal obligation upon the Examining Division to invite observations from the applicant before issuing a decision which adversely affects the applicant.[8] In particular, Article 113(1) EPC provides that a decision may only be based upon grounds or evidence on which a party has had an opportunity to present comments.

In the absence of circumstances which create such a legal obligation to invite further observations, the words "as often as necessary" indicate that the Examining Division has a discretion in each individual case as to whether or not to invite further observations from an applicant before issuing a decision which adversely affects him.[9]

Such discretion should be exercised in favour of inviting further observations if there is a reasonable prospect that such an invitation could lead to the grant of the application. Article 96(2) EPC does not exclude communication with the applicant in other circumstances, but it relieves the Examining Division of any obligation to send communications which on a reasonable, objective basis could be considered superfluous.[10]

The aim of the Examining Division, in accordance with the public interest as well as the interest of individual applicants, is "to carry out the substantive examination thoroughly, efficiently and expeditiously".[11] This aim is, of course, subsidiary to the principle in Article 113(1) EPC set out above.

The interests of orderly and economic examining procedures may preclude the sending of more than one communication where this would not appear to be likely to lead to a positive result. In practice, there must obviously be a limit to the number of opportunities which an applicant should be given to submit further arguments in support of his application, whether or not they are accompanied by proposals to amend the application.

If the applicant fails to make any real progress towards the refutation of the presumption of invalidity properly established in the first communication by the Examining Division, or no such progress appears to be possible even with amendments on the face of the information available, it is within the discretion of the Examining Division to interpret the submissions on behalf of the applicant as complete and final, and to assume, in consequence, that no useful purpose would be served by the provision of further opportunities for filing observations.[12]

It should also be noted that Article 113(1) EPC does not require that the applicant be given a repeated opportunity to comment on the argumenta-

---

[8] T640/91 O.J. EPO 1994, 913.
[9] Ibid., and T84/82 O.J. EPO 1983, 451.
[10] T162/82 O.J. EPO 1987, 533.
[11] T84/82 O.J. EPO 1983, 451.
[12] Ibid.

tion of the Examining Division so long as the decisive objections against the grant of the European patent remain the same.[13]

Nevertheless, when applications are refused after only one opportunity to respond to the objections to grant which have been raised, applicants may consider that the refusal was arbitrary, and that further dialogue might have resolved the situation without recourse to the filing of an appeal.

There are two ways of alleviating this situation open to applicants:

(1) Requesting oral proceedings (as to which see paragraph 2–25, below);

(2) Filing one or more auxiliary requests (see paragraph 2–15, below).[14]

(c) Amendments

The procedural admissibility of an amendment of an application is **2–11** governed by Article 123(1) and Rule 86 EPC. Thus, Article 123(1) EPC sets out an overriding principle that "In any case, an applicant shall be allowed at least one opportunity of amending the description, claims and drawings of his own volition." Beyond this, however, the admissibility of an amendment depends upon the stage of the procedure, as follows:

(i) Before receipt of the European Search Report

Pursuant to Rule 86(1) EPC, no amendment may be made before receipt **2–12** of the European Search Report issued pursuant to Article 92(1) EPC ("except where otherwise provided," *i.e.* in particular, under Rule 41 EPC in order to remedy deficiencies of a formal nature).

(ii) After receipt of the European Search Report

The following opportunities to amend are provided: **2–13**
(a) After receipt of the search report and before receipt of a communication from the Examining Division, amendment is as of right (Rule 86(2) EPC).
(b) Similarly, after receipt of the first communication from the Examining Division, the applicant may amend once as of right at the same time as he replies to such communication (Rule 86(3) EPC).
(c) Thereafter, "no further amendment may be made without the consent of the Examining Division" (Rule 86(3) EPC, second sentence).

(iii) Exercise of discretion to admit amendment

The principles by which such discretion is exercised in practice are **2–14** basically the same in proceedings before the Examining Division and the Boards of Appeal. In particular, it is an overriding principle that an

---

[13] T162/82 O.J. EPO 1987, 533.
[14] T300/89 O.J. EPO 1991, 480.

amendment which is proposed in reply to objections to grant (at any stage of the proceedings) will be accepted provided it is clearly allowable, both formally (*i.e.* having regard to Article 123(2) EPC), and in the sense that it overcomes the objections to patentability which have been raised.

In normal practice, if in reply to a communication from the Examining Division which raises objections to grant the applicant proposes amendments which go a long way towards meeting the objections, a further opportunity to amend will be allowed provided that allowable amendments can be envisaged. It is quite common for allowable amendments to be suggested to applicants for their consideration during pre-grant proceedings.

However, it is also clearly within the discretion of the Examining Division, in a case where one or more proposals to amend have been made in reply to a communication raising objections to grant but where the amendments do not come close to meeting the objections, to issue a decision refusing the application.

In this event, the applicant's only remedy is to appeal.

(iv) Main and auxiliary requests

2–15 The basic practice in relation to the filing of main and auxiliary requests before the Examining Division is set out in Legal Advice No. 15/84:[15] "under Article 113(2) EPC, the EPO is bound by the applicant's submissions: the European patent may be granted only on the basis of a text which is without formal or substantive deficiency [under the EPC], submitted or agreed to by the applicant in its entirety". It follows that if any one claim in a set of claims is disallowable, the complete set of claims (and therefore the application including such set) is disallowable, and must be replaced by a set of claims in which all are allowable.

In order to meet the objections of the Examining Division and in order to obtain the maximum allowable extent of protection, an applicant may file an appropriate number of auxiliary requests in response to a communication raising objections to grant. An auxiliary request is a request for amendment which is contingent upon the main request or preceding auxiliary requests being held to be disallowable.[16]

(d) Divisional applications

(i) Introduction

2–16 After filing a European patent application, an applicant may file a divisional application in respect of subject matter which is divided out of the earlier application. A divisional application may be filed "only in respect of subject matter which does not extend beyond the content of the earlier application as filed" (Article 76(1) EPC). This requirement is the

---

[15] Legal Advice No. 15/84, O.J. EPO 1984, 491.
[16] T153/85 O.J. EPO 1988, 1.

same as that which applies mutatis mutandis to the amendment of an application after filing: see paragraph 7–02, below. The relevant jurisprudence which is applicable to such amendments is also applicable to divisional applications, and vice versa.

A divisional application is "deemed to have been filed on the date of filing of the earlier application and shall have the benefit of any right to priority" (Article 76(1) EPC).

A divisional application may be filed by an applicant either of his own motion, or in order to meet an objection of lack of unity of invention under Aeticle 82 EPC during the examination procedure.

(ii) Time for filing

Under Rule 25(1) EPC, an applicant may file a divisional application at **2–17** any time "up to the approval of the text in accordance with Rule 51(4) EPC in which the European patent is to be granted," but no later.[17]

(e) Applications containing more than one invention

If a European patent application as filed is considered by the Search **2–18** Division as not complying with the requirement of unity of invention set out in Article 82 EPC a partial European search report is drawn up on the subject matter of the invention which is first mentioned in the claims; and the applicant is informed that if the search report is to cover other inventions which are in the application, and additional search fee must be paid for each such invention (Rule 46(1) EPC).

Payment of additional search fees as so requested ensures that after receipt of the search report, the applicant may choose which invention to put forward in the claims of the application, and may file divisional applications in respect of the other inventions which have been covered by the search report.

If the applicant has paid further search fees as requested by the Search Division he may subsequently request a refund from the Examining Division (or from the Board of Appeal in any appeal) on the basis that the finding of non-unity of invention by the Search Division was not justified (Rule 46(2) EPC).

An applicant who fails to pay further search fees in response to a request under Rule 46(1) EPC from the Search Division cannot pursue that application for the subject matter in respect of which no search fees have been paid. Such an applicant must file a divisional application in respect of such subject matter if he wishes to seek protection for it.[18]

(f) Withdrawal of an application

(i) Introduction

Withdrawal of an application is envisaged in Article 67(4) EPC, where it **2–19** is provided that the effect of withdrawal is retrospective in that the application is deemed never to have conferrred any protection upon the

---

[17] G10/92 O.J. EPO 1994, 633.
[18] G2/92 1993, 591.

applicant under Article 64 EPC (*i.e.* from the date of publication). Furthermore, under Rule 92(n) EPC, the date of withdrawal must be entered in the Register of Patents, and under Article 129(a) EPC, this date must be published in the Patent Bulletin, for reasons of legal certainty. Withdrawal of a European patent application is binding on an applicant.[19] Moreover, further processing of an application under Article 121 EPC (see paragraph 5–02, below) is not possible following withdrawal of an application.

(ii) What constitutes a withdrawal?

2–20   Since the withdrawal of an application has such an irreversible effect, it is important to be able to determine when a withdrawal has actually been made. In this connection two possibilities should be distinguished, namely:

(a) "active" withdrawal, which is intended to be immediately effective;

(b) "passive" abandonment, where it is intended that the applicant will take no further action in connection with the application, with the result that the application will in due course lapse through non-payment of a renewal fee.

Each case in which there is a dispute as to the applicant's intentions has to be considered on its own facts.[20] A high degree of certainty is necessary before a statement can properly be interpreted as an active withdrawal. Where there is any doubt as to the actual intent of an applicant, his statement can only be construed as an active withdrawal if the related facts confirm that such was his true intention.[21]

(iii) Retraction of a withdrawal

2–21   Legal Advice No. 8/80 emphasises that the necessity for legal certainty in connection with the withdrawal of an application basically excludes the possibility of retraction of a withdrawal once made.[22]

(g) Abandonment of particular subject matter

2–22   Similar principles apply to abandonment of particular subject matter within a patent application, for example, certain claims and the corresponding description. Thus, if on the true interpretation of a statement made by an applicant or patentee it may be considerted that a particular subject matter has been expressly abandoned together with the complete deletion of the appropriate claim and in addition all support therefore in the specification, such subject matter cannot be reinstated in the application.[23]

---

[19] T153/85 O.J. EPO 1988, 1.

[20] J15/86 O.J. EPO 1988, 417; see also J11/80 O.J. EPO 1981, 141; J6/86 O.J. EPO 1988, 124; J7/87 O.J. EPO 1988, 422.

[21] J11/87 O.J. EPO 1988, 367.

[22] Legal Advice No. 8/80 O.J. EPO 1981, 6; see also J15/86 O.J. EPO 1988, 417.

[23] T61/85 [1988] EPOR 20.

Furthermore, if an applicant cancels claims included in a European patent application, with a view to the filing of a divisional application in respect of the subject matter of such claims, he should at the time of cancellation state that the cancellation is without prejudice to the filing of a divisional application.[24]

D. OBSERVATIONS BY THIRD PARTIES

Article 115 EPC provides that any person may file observations in **2–23** writing concerning the patentability of an invention which is the subject of a European patent application, following publication of the application. The observations must include the grounds on which they are based. A person who files such observations is not a party to the examination proceedings before the EPO.

Any such observations are communicated to the applicant, who may comment upon them. The EPO may of its own motion take up the contents of such observations as objections to the grant of a patent, under Article 114(1) EPC.

The procedure under Article 115 EPC may in particular be useful if a competitor of the applicant knows of grounds of objection to a patent application which are not known to the EPO, and wishes such grounds to be considered by the EPO without having to wait for possible grant of the patent and the consequent opportunity to commence opposition proceedings.

E. SUSPENSION OF EXAMINATION PROCEEDINGS

(a) Pending Enlarged Board of Appeal proceedings

Whenever a decision of the Examining Division depends entirely on the **2–24** outcome of proceedings before the Enlarged Board of Appeal on a legal question or point of law raised according to Article 112 EPC — and this is known to the Examining Division — the further examination of the application is suspended until the matter is decided by the Enlarged Board of Appeal.[25]

(b) Pending proceedings concerning entitlement to grant

Rule 13(1) EPC provides for suspension of examination proceedings if a third party provides proof to the EPO that he has opened proceedings against the applicant for the purpose of seeking a judgment that he is entitled to the grant of the European patent. The EPO "shall stay the proceedings" unless the third party consents to continuation.

---

[24] J15/85 O.J. EPO 1986, 395.
[25] T166/84 O.J. EPO 1984, 489.

Rule 13(3) EPC provides that the EPO may set a date for continuing the examination proceedings, which may subsequently be varied.[26]

F. ORAL PROCEEDINGS

2–25   The procedure in connection with the appointment of oral proceedings pursuant to Article 116 EPC is fully discussed in paragraphs 4–38 *et seq.*, below. These procedural principles are also applicable to proceedings before the Examining Divisions.

G. PREPARATION FOR GRANT: LATE REQUESTS FOR AMENDMENT

2–26   Before granting a patent, the Examining Division must inform the applicant of the proposed text in which it intends to grant the patent, and it must request the applicant's approval of such text, within a fixed period of between two and four months, which shall be extended once by up to two months upon request (Rule 51(4) EPC). If no approval is communicated to the Examining Division in due time, the application is refused (Rule 51(5) EPC).

After the Rule 51(4) EPC communication has been issued, amendments to the text may still be requested under Rule 86(3) EPC, within the fixed period. If the Examining Division does not consent to amendments requested during this period, it must give its reasons, and it must invite the applicant to submit observations within a specified period, before taking its decision (Rule 51(5) EPC).

If, following a Rule 51(4() EPC communication the applicant gives his approval to the proposed text within the fixed period, and subsequently, but still within the fixed period, he withdraws such approval and requests amendments to the text, such requested amendments must be considered by the Examining Division under Rule 51(5) EPC: and in the absence of an approved text, the application cannot proceed to grant.[27]

After approval of the text pursuant to a Rule 51(4) EPC communication, the applicant is invited to pay fees for grant and printing and to file translations of the claims into the other two official languages, with a non-extendable fixed period of between two and three months (Rule 51(6) EPC). Failure to comply with such a request within the fixed period results in the application being deemed to be withdrawn (Rule 51(8) EPC).

An approval of a notified text by an applicant under Rule 51(4) EPC is not binding, even after a communication in accordance with Rule 51(6) EPC has been issued. The Examining Division has a discretion under Rule 86(3) EPC to allow amendment of an application up until it decides to grant a patent under Article 97(2) EPC. After issue of a communication under Rule 51(6) EPC the allowance of a request for amendment will be

---

[26] T146/82 O.J. EPO 1985, 267.
[27] T1/92 O.J. EPO 1993, 685.

an exception rather than the rule, however.[28] Up until the decision to grant, an obvious mistake may be corrected under Rule 88 EPC.[29]

As to the latest date for filing a divisional application, see paragraph 2–17 above.

The decision to grant a patent must state the text which forms the basis of the grant (Rule 51(11) EPC), and takes effect on the date on which the European Patent Bulletin mentions the grant (Article 97(4) EPC).

H. RIGHT TO A EUROPEAN PATENT: THE LAWFUL APPLICANT

The right to a European patent belongs to the inventor or his successor **2–27** in title (Article 60 EPC). Prior to grant, a dispute as to who has the right to a European patent in respect of an invention is decided by the appropriate national court in accordance with the Protocol on Recognition,[30] which is an integral part of the EPC. Article 61 EPC governs subsequent procedure before the EPO, when a person other than the applicant is judged by a national court to be entitled to the grant. Such lawful applicant may file a new application for a patent at the EPO under Article 61(1)(b) EPC, even if an earlier application by the unlawful applicant is no longer pending.[31]

---

[28] G7/93 O.J. EPO 1994, 775.
[29] T675/90 O.J. EPO 1994, 58.
[30] Protocol on Jurisdiction and the Recognition of Decisions in respect of the right to the grant of a European Patent.
[31] G3/92 O.J. EPO 1994, 607.

3. Opposition Procedure

Contents

A. INTRODUCTION

The procedure which should be followed by the Opposition Divisions is **3–01** dealt with comprehensively in the Guidelines. The EPO has also published guidance entitled *Opposition Procedure in the EPO*.[1]

When a European patent is granted, it becomes a bundle of national patents in the designated Contracting States: each such patent is independently governed by the law of its Contracting State: see paragraphs 1–04 and 1–12. The proprietor has the same rights as would be conferred by a national patent granted in each such State. Thus, upon grant of a European patent, there is a transfer of competence in respect of the rights which are conferred by it from the EPO to the designated Contracting States, who are thereafter responsible for its administration and enforcement.

Opposition proceedings constitute an exception to this general rule of transfer of competence. The opposition procedure under Articles 99 to 105 EPC is a post-grant opposition procedure whereby, during a limited period of time (namely nine months from grant), a centralised action for revocation of the complete bundle of national patents constituting the European patent may be brought before and decided by the EPO.[2]

The cost and time advantages of such a centralised revocation procedure as compared to separate revocation proceedings in the national courts of Contracting States are of obvious practical significance.

When infringement proceedings have been commenced before a national court in respect of a European patent which is the subject of opposition

---

[1] O.J. EPO 1989, 471.
[2] See, *e.g.* T117/86 O.J. EPO 1989, 401; T9/87 O.J. EPO 1989, 438.

proceedings before the EPO, such an opposition will receive accelerated processing, so far as procedural rules allow.[3]

B. NATURE OF OPPOSITION PROCEEDINGS

3–02   The different nature of the opposition procedure, as compared to the pre-grant examination, was emphasised by the Enlarged Board of Appeal, in a statement in one of its early decisions that "opposition procedure is not designed to be, and is not to be misused as, an extension of examination procedure".[4]

Furthermore, "the opposition procedure is an independent procedure which takes place after the grant procedure; it is a separate procedure in which a patent wrongly granted may be limited or revoked . . . the opposition procedure is not part of the grant procedure".[5]

Like examination procedure, the opposition procedure is a purely administrative procedure.[6]

The Enlarged Board of Appeal has emphasised that "opposition proceedings under the EPC are in principle to be considered as contentious proceedings between parties normally representing opposite interests, who should be given equally fair treatment; furthermore, it is inherent in any post-grant opposition procedure that the competence of the patent office to deal with the patent depends on the action taken by the opponent".[7] This matter is considered further in paragraphs 3–30 and 3–31 below.

C. COMPOSITION OF AN OPPOSITION DIVISION

(a) Relationship with members of the Examining Division

3–03   The appointment of members to form an Opposition Division to decide upon a particular case is governed by Article 19(2) EPC: at least two of the three examiners "shall not have taken part in the proceedings for grant of the patent to which the opposition relates"; furthermore, an examiner who has taken part in such examination proceedings "shall not be the Chairman". In certain cases, an Opposition Division may also include a legally qualified examiner, "if the nature of the decision so requires". For example, a legally qualified examiner is normally included if oral evidence is to be taken.

If the composition of an Opposition Division is contrary to Article 19(2) EPC, its decision may be held to be void, and the case ordered to be reheard before a properly constituted Opposition Division.[8]

---

[3] Notice of the EPO dated June 11, 1990, O.J. EPO 1990, 324.
[4] G1/84 O.J. EPO 1985, 299.
[5] T198/88 O.J. EPO 1991, 254.
[6] G7, 8/91 O.J. EPO 1993, 346 and 356.
[7] G9, 10/91 O.J. EPO 1993, 408 and 420.
[8] T251/88 [1990] EPOR 246.

(b) Suspected partiality of a member of the Opposition Division

Although Article 24 EPC sets out the requirement of impartiality of members of the Boards of Appeal only, the same requirement applies to the first instance departments of the EPO, in particular the Opposition Divisions. A decision of an Opposition Division may be challenged in an appeal on the ground of suspected partiality.[9] Disqualifying partiality presumes a preconceived attitude on the part of a member towards a party in an case.[10] **3–04**

D. FILING AN OPPOSITION

(a) Who may file an opposition?

(i) Any person

Any person may file a notice of opposition to a European patent, *i.e.* any natural or legal person (Article 99(1) EPC). There is no requirement that an opponent must show an interest in the subject matter of the patent. **3–05**

(ii) The patent proprietor: no self-opposition

An earlier decision of the Enlarged Board of Appeal[11] which held that a patent proprietor may file an opposition against his own patent has been overruled by the Enlarged Board in a later decision.[12] Such a "self-opposition" is therefore inadmissible. **3–06**

(iii) A professional representative

A professional representative may file an opposition in his own name on his own behalf,[13] but not when he is in fact acting in his professional capacity on behalf of a client; in such circumstances, the notice of opposition does not comply with Rule 55(a) and (d) EPC.[14] **3–07**

(iv) Identity of the opponent

The true identity of the opponent must be clear. Article 99(1) EPC gives to any person a personal action at law to oppose a patent. An opposition instituted by a person acting with the personal action at law of someone else is prohibited, and is therefore inadmissible,[15] – for example, if the **3–08**

---

[9] G5/91 O.J. EPO 1992, 617.
[10] T261/88 February 16, 1993.
[11] G1/84 O.J. EPO 1985, 299.
[12] G9/93 O.J. EPO 1994, 891.
[13] T635/88 O.J. EPO 1993, 608.
[14] T10/82 O.J. EPO 1983, 407.
[15] T635/88 O.J. EPO 1993, 608.

person filing the opposition is a professional representative acting on behalf of a client.[16] If doubt exists as to the true identity of the opponent, the opposition is inadmissible (see paragraph 3–15 below).

(b) Representation of an opponent

3–09   The same provisions of Article 133 EPC apply to the representation of an opponent as to an applicant in proceedings before the EPO (see paragraph 2–05 above); that is, an opponent who does not have either a residence or a place of business within the territory of one of the Contracting States must be represented by a professional representative and must act through him in the opposition proceedings.

(c) Time limit for filing opposition

3–10   In order to comply with the requirements of Article 99 and Rule 55 EPC, a notice of opposition must be filed within nine months "from the publication of the mention of the grant of the European patent" (Article 99(1) EPC), which is in effect the date of grant of the patent by virtue of Article 97(4) EPC.

The final sentence of Article 99(1) EPC provides that the notice of opposition "shall not be deemed to have been filed until the opposition fee has been paid". If the opposition fee is not paid within the nine-month period, the opposition is inadmissible.[17]

(d) Place of filing

3–11   A notice of opposition may be filed at the EPO filing offices in Munich, The Hague, or Berlin.[18]

(e) Language

3–12   The official language of the EPO (English, French or German) in which a European patent application is filed becomes the "language of the proceedings" for all subsequent proceedings before the EPO concerning that application or any resulting European patent (Article 14(3) EPC). Nevertheless, in written proceedings any party may use any official language (Rule 1(1) EPC). Thus, a notice of opposition may be filed in English, French or German.

Furthermore, in accordance with Article 14(2) and (4) EPC, "natural or legal persons having their residence or principal place of business" within a Contracting State having a language other than English, French or German as an official language may file documents which have to be filed

---

[16] T10/82 O.J. EPO 1983, 407.
[17] T152/85 O.J. EPO 1987, 191.
[18] For Berlin, see the Decision of the President of the EPO, May 10, 1989, O.J. EPO 1989, 218.

within a time limit (such as a notice of opposition) in that official language (for example, an Italian resident may file a notice of opposition in Italian). However, a translation into one of the three official languages of the EPO must then be filed within a prescribed period (Rule 6(2) EPC) although it may accompany the notice of opposition.[19] If the translation is not filed in due time, the notice of opposition is deemed not to have been received, and the opposition fee is refunded.[20] It is the residence or principal place of business of the opponent that is decisive, not that of the opponent's professional representative.[21]

Rule 6(3) EPC provides a 20 per cent reduction in the opposition fee to an opponent who files a notice of opposition pursuant to Article 14(2) and (4) EPC in such a language.

E. Transfer of an Opposition

(a) By assignment

An opposition pending before the EPO may be transferred or assigned **3–13** to a third party as part of the opponent's business assets together with the assets in the interests of which the opposition was filed.[22]

(b) To an heir or successor in title

The transmission of an opposition to the opponent's heirs is acknowledged implicitly in Rule 60(2) EPC which stipulates that the opposition proceedings may be continued even without the participation of the deceased opponent's heirs.[23] By analogy, an opposition may also be transmitted to the opponent's universal successor in law.[24]

F. Contents of the Notice of Opposition: Admissibility

The basic requirement for a notice of opposition in accordance with **3–14** Article 99(1) EPC is that it must be "a written reasoned statement". Beyond this, Rule 55 EPC prescribes certain particulars which every notice must contain. These may be divided into two categories, according to whether or not such contents must be included in the notice within the nine-month opposition period for the notice to be held admissible under Rule 56(1) EPC.

(a) Contents which are essential within the nine month-period

(i) Identity of the opponent

As discussed in paragraph 3–05 above, Article 99(1) EPC provides that **3–15** "any person" may file a notice of opposition within the nine-month period. If the identity of an opponent has not been established before

[19] G6/91 O.J. EPO 1992, 491.
[20] T193/87 O.J. EPO 1993, 207.
[21] T149/85 O.J. EPO 1986, 103.
[22] G4/88 O.J. EPO 1989, 480.
[23] *Ibid.*
[24] *Ibid.*

expiry of the period allowed for opposition (see paragraph 3–08 above), the opposition is inadmissible.[25]

This conclusion is not immediately obvious from the literal wording of Rules 55 and 56 EPC, if read in isolation.

(ii) Identity of the opposed patent

3–16   The first sentence of Article 99(1) EPC provides for notice of opposition "to the European patent granted" within the nine-month period. Furthermore, Rule 55(b) provides that the notice of opposition shall contain "the number of the (opposed) European patent . . . , and the name of the proprietor and title of the invention." Rule 55(1) EPC makes a notice of opposition inadmissible if within the nine-month period it "does not provide sufficient identification of the (opposed) patent."

The particulars in the notice of opposition should enable the EPO, without undue effort, to identify with certainty the contested patent before expiry of the opposition period.[26]

This is a question of fact to be determined in each individual case. Particulars in the notice other than those specified in Rule 55(b) EPC may be used to aid such identification.[27]

(iii) Extent to which the patent is opposed

3–17   Rule 55(c) EPC requires the notice of opposition to contain "a statement of the extent to which the European patent is opposed"; for example, the number of claims which are opposed. Thus, it should be clear from the notice whether the opposition is directed against the entire patent or only a part of it.

(iv) Grounds of opposition and support

3–18   Rule 55(c) EPC further requires that the notice of opposition contains a statement of:

(a) "the grounds on which the opposition is based";
(b) "an indication of the facts, evidence and arguments presented in support of the grounds".

3–19 Grounds.   The only possible grounds of opposition are set out in Article 100 EPC, namely:

(a) the subject matter is not patentable, under Articles 52 to 57 EPC; therefore including:

(i) excluded subject matter, Articles 52 and 53 EPC;
(ii) lack of novelty, Article 54 EPC;

---

[25] T25/85 O.J. EPO 1986, 81.
[26] T317/86 O.J. EPO 1989, 378.
[27] *Ibid.*

(iii) lack of inventive step, Article 56 EPC;
(iv) not susceptible of industrial application, Article 57 EPC;
(b) insufficiency of disclosure, under Article 83 EPC;
(c) addition of subject matter, under Article 123(2) EPC.

It should be noted that the requirements of Article 84 EPC ("clarity" and "support", see paragraphs 6–30 to 6–33) do not constitute a ground of opposition.

Indication of facts, evidence and arguments in support: substantiation. The intention of Article 99(1) and Rule 55(c) EPC in combination is to ensure that the notice of opposition as filed within the prescribed nine-month period summarises the entire case of the opponent as to why the European patent should not be maintained in its form as granted. The notice of opposition should state the legal and factual reasons why the alleged grounds of opposition should succeed.[28] If the only facts and evidence indicated in a notice of opposition cannot as a matter of law support the grounds of opposition alleged, the opposition is inadmissible. In such a case the notice of opposition necessarily contains nothing which could possibly lead to the patent being revoked.[29]

3–20

The requirement under Rule 55(c) EPC is only satisfied if the contents of the notice of opposition are sufficient for the opponent's case to be properly understood on an objective basis,[30] both by the patent proprietor and by the Opposition Division, without further investigations.[31]

If none of the alleged grounds of opposition is properly substantiated in the manner set out above, the opposition is inadmissible. If at least one of the alleged grounds (or the only alleged ground) is properly substantiated, the opposition is admissible.

The requirement for substantiation under Rule 55(c) EPC has the double function of:

(i) governing the admissibility of the opposition;
(ii) establishing the legal and factual framework within which the substantive examination of the opposition shall be conducted.[32]

The extent to which grounds of opposition which have been alleged but not substantiated are examined during the opposition proceedings is considered in paragraph 3–31 below.

Substantiation of prior use. When an opposition is based on prior use, the requirements of Rule 55(c) EPC are only fulfilled if the notice of opposition indicates, within the opposition period, all the facts which make it possible to determine the date of prior use, what has been used, and the circumstances relating to the prior use. Prior public use is only adequately substantiated if specific details are given of what was made

3–21

---

[28] T550/88 O.J. EPO 1992, 117.
[29] *Ibid.*
[30] T222/85 O.J. EPO 1988, 128.
[31] T2/89 O.J. EPO 1991, 51.
[32] G9, 10/91 O.J. EPO 1993, 408 and 420.

available to the public, where, when, how and by whom.[33] The notice of opposition must also indicate the evidence and arguments in support of this ground.[34]

However, Rule 55(c) EPC does not require that the facts, evidence and arguments have to be filed during the nine-month opposition period.[35]

3–22   The following are a number of examples concerning admissibility.

(a) A number of prior published documents were relied upon in support of the grounds of lack of novelty and inventive step, each apparently disclosing some of the claimed combination of features in the opposed patent. The notice of opposition did not make clear how or why the alleged grounds should succeed, and was therefore inadmissible.[36]

(b) The only alleged ground of opposition was lack of novelty under Article 54(3) EPC, and this ground was supported only by reference to a document constituting a "national prior right" (see paragraph 10–13), which is not a prior right within the meaning of Article 54(3) EPC. Since the opposition could not succeed on this basis as a matter of law, it was held inadmissible.[37]

(c) The only alleged ground of opposition was lack of inventive step, and the only patent document supporting this was not prior published, and therefore not within the state of the art (see paragraph 10–04). Nevertheless, the document identified on its front page another patent document having exactly the same contents, which had been prior published. The opposition was held admissible.[38]

In order to expedite proceedings, parties should, in principle, submit all facts, evidence and requests at the beginning of the procedure. Where this is not possible, the facts, evidence or requests must be submitted at the earliest opportunity. If relevant facts or evidence are submitted by a party only at a late stage of proceedings without very good reason and if as a consequence unnecessary costs are incurred by another party, this will be taken into account in apportionment of costs (see paragraph 4–47 below).[39]

The underlying principle is one of early and complete presentation of the case as opposed to the piecemeal and tardy introduction of the arguments and supporting evidence.[40]

(b) Contents which are not essential within the nine-month period

3–23   Rule 55 EPC requires that a notice contains:

---

[33] T93/89 O.J. EPO 1992, 718.
[34] T328/87 O.J. EPO 1992, 701.
[35] *Ibid.*
[36] T222/85 O.J. EPO 1988, 128.
[37] T550/88 O.J. EPO 1992, 117.
[38] T185/88 O.J. EPO 1990, 451.
[39] "Opposition procedure in the EPO", O.J. EPO 1989, 417.
[40] T326/87 O.J. EPO 1992, 522.

(a) "the name and address of the opponent"; and "the State in which his residence or principal place of business is located" (in accordance with Rule 26(2)(c) EPC).

These requirements are clearly primarily for the purpose of further identification of the opponent, as well as in order that it can be decided whether the opponent requires a professional representative (see paragraph 3–09, above).

(b) "the number of the (opposed) European patent"; "the name of the proprietor"; "the title of the invention".

Again, these requirements are primarily for the purpose of identification of the opposed patent and its proprietor.

If such requirements are noted as not complied with, the deficiencies may be remedied within a period fixed by the Opposition Division, which may expire outside the nine-month limit. Failure to correct the deficiencies wiithin the fixed period will result in the opposition being rejected as inadmissible.

G. Examination of a Notice of Opposition for Admissibility

When a notice of opposition is first filed, it is formally examined for **3–24** admissibility in respect of all matters except those set out in Rule 55(c) EPC by a Formalities Officer of the Opposition Division. In the case of deficiencies (see paragraph 3–23 above), a communication may be sent under Rule 56 EPC, and a decision rejecting the opposition as inadmissible may be issued, on an *ex parte* basis.

In the event that the notice of opposition is not rejected as inadmissible under Rule 56 EPC, it is communicated to the proprietor under Rule 57(1) EPC and the patent proprietor may then contest the admissibility of the opposition in his observations in reply. Such contentions, including inadmissibility under Rule 55(c) EPC, are decided in *inter partes* proceedings by the Opposition Division itself.

The fact that the opposition is not rejected as inadmissible on an *ex parte* basis does not in any way preclude a finding of inadmissibility during the *inter partes* proceedings.[41]

The admissibility of an opposition is an essential prerequisite for its substantive examination. When an opposition is held inadmissible, its substance cannot be examined.[42]

H. Preparation for Substantive Examination

Following the filing of a notice of opposition and its preliminary **3–25** examination for admissibility, the case is prepared for the examination stage. This preparation is governed by Rule 57 EPC. Thus:

---

[41] T222/85 O.J. EPO 1988, 128.
[42] T328/87 O.J. EPO 1992, 701; T925/91 O.J. EPO (P).

(a) The notice of opposition is sent to the patent proprietor, and he is invited to file observations and/or amendments to the text of the patent where appropriate, within a fixed period.

(b) In the case of several opponents filing notices of opposition, each notice is sent to the other opponents.

(c) Any observations and amendments filed by the patent proprietor in response to the invitation under (a) are sent to all opponents, who are invited to reply to the patent proprietor's submissions within a fixed period if the Opposition Division "considers it expedient" (Rule 57(3) EPC).

I. Substantive Examination of an Opposition

Procedure during the examination stage before the Opposition Division is governed by Article 101(2) and Rule 57 and 58 EPC.

(a) Observations by the parties

3–26   An Opposition Division has the power under Article 101(2) and Rule 57 EPC to control the extent of the observations filed by parties during the examination of an opposition.[43]

Following the late filing of new evidence by an opponent, if the EPO intends to consider such evidence in view of its relevance to the decision to be taken, then in the absence of observations upon such evidence by the patent proprietor, it is necessary within the meaning of Article 101(2) EPC to invite the proprietor to present his comments by filing observations, before the case can be decided on the basis of such evidence. This follows both from Article 113(1) EPC and from the general principles of procedural law applicable under Article 125 EPC.[44]

(b) The content of communications

3–27   Preliminary expressions of opinion by the Opposition Division are often included in communications for the purposes of clarifying and expediting the proceedings.

(c) Amendments to the patent

(i) Amendment must be appropriate

3–28   Rule 57(1) EPC requires that when a notice of opposition is communicated to the patentee, the Opposition Division shall invite him to file amendments, where appropriate, to the description, claims and drawings within a fixed period.

---

[43] T295/87 O.J. EPO 1990, 470.
[44] T669/90 O.J. EPO 1992, 739.

Thereafter, Rule 58(2) EPC provides that in any communication to the patentee "he shall, where appropriate, be invited to file, where necessary, the description, claims and drawings in amended form."

Under Rule 57a EPC, which comes into force on June 1, 1995, "the description, claims and drawings may be amended, provided that the amendments are occasioned by grounds of opposition specified in Article 100 EPC, even if the respective ground has not been invoked by the opponent." Earlier practice limiting the scope of allowable amendments during opposition proceedings is thus suspended.[45]

The allowability of proposals to amend a patent is a matter of discretion under the above Rules.

(ii) Auxiliary requests

An auxiliary request is a request for amendment which is contingent **3–29** upon the main request, or preceding main and auxiliary requests, being held to be unallowable.[46] In response to an opposition a patentee may submit a main request (*e.g.* that the patent be maintained as granted), and an appropriate number of auxiliary requests (*e.g.* with more restricted main claims).[47]

(e) Extent of the substantive examination

(i) The extent to which the patent is opposed

In most oppositions the opponent states that the entire extent of the **3–30** patent is the subject of the opposition proceedings. Nevertheless, occasionally a notice of opposition states that only certain speciified claims (*i.e.* specified subject matter) of the patent are opposed.

In this circumstance the power of an Opposition Division (and a Board of Appeal) to examine and decide upon the maintenance of the patent under Articles 101 and 102 EPC depends upon the extent to which the patent has been opposed. Subject matter within the patent which is not opposed in the notice of opposition is not the subject of the opposition proceedings, and the EPO therefore has no competence of power to deal with such subject matter.[48]

However, if such opposed claims cannot be maintained as a result of the grounds of opposition, claims which are dependent on the opposed claims may also be examined in the opposition proceedings if their validity is prima facie also in doubt.[49]

(ii) The grounds of opposition to be examined

If the opponent only states certain of the grounds of opposition set out **3–31** in Article 100(a), (b) and (c) EPC, the question also arises as to whether, and if so in what circumstances, an Opposition Division (or a Board of

---

[45] T406/86 O.J. EPO 1989, 302, T295/87 O.J. EPO 1990, 470, T127/85 O.J. EPO 1989, 271.
[46] T153/85 O.J. EPO 1988, 1.
[47] T234/86 O.J. EPO 1989, 79.
[48] G9/91 O.J. EPO 1993, 408; T9/87 O.J. EPO 1989, 438; T293/88 O.J. EPO 1992, 220.
[49] G9/91 O.J. EPO 1993, 408; T293/88 O.J. EPO 1992, 220.

Appeal, as to which, see paragraph 4–32) can examine and decide upon the validity of the opposed patent having regard to other grounds of opposition than those stated by the opponent.

An Opposition Division is not obliged to consider grounds which are not relied upon in the notice of opposition. In principle, the Opposition Division should examine only those grounds of opposition which have been alleged and properly substantiated in the notice of opposition. Exceptionally, an Opposition Division may apply Article 114(1) EPC and consider other grounds of opposition which prima facie appear to prejudice maintenance of the patent.[50]

(iii) Examination of late-filed facts and evidence

3–32 In order to expedite proceedings, parties should submit the facts and evidence on which they rely, together with their requests, at the beginning of the opposition proceedings. An Opposition Division may disregard facts or evidence which are not filed in due time (Article 114(2) EPC).[51] However, facts or evidence which are crucial to the decision in the sense that they may affect the result are normally admitted into the proceedings even if filed at a late stage.[52] Costs may then be awarded[53] (see paragraph 4–47).

Late-filed facts, evidence and related arguments which go beyond the "indication of facts, evidence and arguments" presented in the notice of opposition pursuant to Rule 55(c) EPC should only exceptionally be admitted into the proceedings, if prima facie there are clear reasons to suspect that such late-filed material would prejudice maintenance of the opposed patent[54] (cf. paragraph 4–33 below concerning appeal proceedings).

(iv) Examination of objections arising from amendments

3–33 Article 102(3) EPC provides that "If the Opposition Division is of the opinion that (in view of the amendments made during the opposition proceedings) the patent and the invention to which it relates meet the requirements of the EPC", it shall maintain the patent as amended.

In all cases in which amendments are requested by the patentee and are considered to be free from objection under Article 123 EPC, Article 102(3) EPC confers upon the Opposition Division (and the Board of Appeal) jurisdiction, and thus the power, to decide upon the patent as amended in the light of the requirements of the EPC as a whole. This jurisdiction is thus wider than that conferred by Articles 102(1) and (2) EPC, which expressly limit jurisdiction to the grounds of opposition mentioned in Article 100 EPC. When substantive amendments are made to a patent

---

[50] G10/91 O.J. EPO 1993, 420.
[51] "Opposition Procedure in the EPO", O.J. EPO 1989, 417.
[52] T156/84 O.J. EPO 1988, 372.
[53] See, e.g. T117/86 O.J. EPO 1989, 401.
[54] T1002/92 O.J. EPO (P).

within the extent to which the patent is opposed, both instances have the power to deal with grounds and issues arising from those amendments even though not specifically raised by an opponent pursuant to Rule 55(c) EPC.[55]

Article 102(3) EPC requires consideration as to whether the amendments introduce any contravention of any requirement of the EPC, including Article 84 EPC. Article 102(3) EPC does not allow objections to be based upon Article 84 EPC if such objections do not arise out of the amendments.[56]

The requirement of unity of invention under Article 82 EPC is not one of the "requirements of the EPC" which the amended patent must meet.[57]

(v) Effect of withdrawal of an opposition

By Rule 60(2) EPC, "opposition proceedings may be continued by the **3–34** EPO of its own motion" if an opposition is withdrawn.

After withdrawal of an opposition, the opposition proceedings should be continued by an Opposition Division if they have reached such a state that they are likely to result in a limitation or revocation of the European patent without further assistance from the opponent and without the Opposition Division itself having to undertake extensive investigations.[58]

An Opposition Division should, in principle, continue opposition proceedings when a communication pursuant to Rule 58(4) EPC stating its intention to maintain the patent in amended form was already sent to the parties before the opposition was withdrawn.[59]

As to withdrawal of an opposition by an appellant during appeal proceedings, see paragraph 4–36 below.

(f) Evidence

(i) Written evidence

Under Article 117 EPC, a very broad power is given to the EPO as **3–35** regards the form which evidence may take in proceedings before it. There are no rules as to the form or content of evidence.

Evidence is evaluated in accordance with the principle of free appreciation of means of proof, *i.e.* all documents are admissible as evidence, and the probative value of each document depends upon the circumstances of each particular case.[60]

Cases are commonly decided simply upon the written submissions from the parties, which may include information statements of an evidential nature. An Opposition Division (or a Board of Appeal), in deciding each

---

[55] T227/88 O.J. EPO 1990, 292.
[56] T301/87 O.J. EPO 1990, 335.
[57] G1/91 O.J. EPO 1992, 253.
[58] T197/88 O.J. EPO 1989, 412.
[59] *Ibid.*
[60] T482/89 O.J. EPO 1992, 646.

case, will give such weight (if any) as it considers appropriate to all the evidence which is before it.

(ii) Oral evidence

3–36   At to oral evidence in proceedings before the EPO, this is governed by Article 117(3) to (6) and Rules 72 to 76 EPC. In particular, in accordance with Rule 72 EPC, and the EPO must decide whether it "considers it necessary to hear the oral evidence of parties, witnesses or experts . . .". The decision must set out *inter alia* the investigation to be carried out and relevant facts to be proved.

At the discretion of the EPO such oral evidence may be given, either:

(a) before the first instance department or Board of Appeal,
    or
(b) before a competent court of the country of residence of the person concerned.

The principle of free appreciation of means of proof applies equally to oral evidence.[61]

Before the EPO.   In normal circumstances, the EPO would initially wish to hear the person concerned itself, in which case a summons is issued to the witness to appear before the EPO. However, upon receipt of such a summons, the witness may request that his evidence should be heard by a competent court in his country of residence.

In this circumstance, and also if the EPO receives no reply to its summons, the EPO may request the competent court to take the witness's evidence (Article 117(4) EPC).

Furthermore, if a witness gives evidence before the EPO, the EPO may "if it considers it advisable" request such a competent court to re-examine the evidence given "under oath or in an equally binding form" (Article 117(5) EPC).

Before a competent court.   The procedure for requesting a competent court to take oral evidence on behalf of the EPO is set out in Article 131(2) EPC.

When the EPO makes such a request, it may also request the court to take the evidence "on oath or in an equally binding form".

Similarly, the EPO may request the court "to permit a member of the department concerned to attend the hearing and question the party, witness or expert either through the intermediary of the court or directly" (Article 117(6) EPC.

Underlying these provisions of the EPC is the fact that the EPO does not have authority to administer oaths such as are normally administered to a witness giving evidence before a national court. Thus, in the event that a person gives false evidence before the EPO, no direct sanction is possible. Reference to a competent national court under the procedure discussed above provides an indirect sanction.

---

[61] *Ibid.*

(iii) The standard and burden of proof

Standard of proof. In relation to an issue of fact, the EPO must decide 3–37 what happened, having regard to the available evidence, on the balance of probabilities: *i.e.* it must decide what is more likely than not to have happened.[62]

This applies when the issue in question is purely one of fact, for example, when a document was first made available to the public.

Burden of proof. If the parties to opposition proceedings make contrary assertions which they cannot substantiate and the EPO is unable to establish the facts of its own motion, the patent proprietor is given the benefit of the doubt, because the opponent has failed to prove his case.[63]

(iv) Confidential material

Documents and evidence filed during opposition proceedings before the 3–38 EPO are normally open to inspection by the public upon request (Article 128(4) EPC). A request that documents so filed should be excluded from file inspection is decided by the President of the EPO under Rule 93 EPC.

If a request for exclusion of certain documents (marked "confidential") from file inspection is rejected by the President, such documents are returned to the party who filed them, without examination by the Opposition Division or Board of Appeal.[64]

Documents filed by a party during opposition proceedings by mistake, and in breach of a confidentiality agreement arising out of national court proceedings concerning the opposing party, may be removed from the opposition file and returned unexamined to the party who filed them.[65]

(g) Oral proceedings

The procedure in connection with the appointment of oral proceedings 3–39 pursuant ot Article 116 EPC is fully discussed in relation to appeal proceedings – see paragraphs 4–38 *et seq.* The procedural principles set out there are also applicable in proceedings before the Opposition Divisions.

J. THE DECISION

(a) Kinds of decision

The final outcome of opposition proceedings will involve one of three 3–40 possibilities:

---

[62] T381/87 O.J. EPO 1990, 213; T182/89 O.J. EPO 1991, 391.
[63] T219/83 O.J. EPO 1986, 211.
[64] T516/89 O.J. EPO 1992, 436.
[65] T760/89 O.J. EPO 1994, 797.

(a) the patent may be revoked (Article 102(1) EPC);

(b) the opposition may be rejected, and the patent maintained unamended (Article 102(2) EPC);

(c) the patent may be maintained in amended form (Article 102(3) EPC).

However, decisions which are in effect of an interlocutory nature are commonly issued before an opposition is finally disposed of. For example, an Opposition Division may issue a decision refusing amendment of the patent as requested by the proprietor, on the basis of Article 123(2) EPC (prohibition of added subject matter – see paragraphs 7–02 *et seq.*, below), and thus revoking the patent as having no valid text. This decision may be the subject of an appeal, and if such appeal is allowed, the Opposition Division may proceed with examination of other grounds of opposition (*e.g.* lack of inventive step). Costs may be apportioned in opposition proceedings, under Article 104 EPC (see Guidelines D–IX and paragraph 4–47).

(b) Oral and written decisions

3–41   If requested, oral proceedings will be appointed in respect of such intermediary matters, as well as before the final decision is issued by the Opposition Division in respect of the proceedings.

According to Rule 68 EPC, the decision of an Opposition Division may be announced orally when oral proceedings are held. The written decision is then subsequently notified to the parties.

(c) Finality of an oral decision

3–42   If a decision is announced orally in respect of one or more issues arising in an opposition, such a decision is final in respect of the issues decided, and therefore, cannot thereafter be changed by the same instance, *i.e.* by the Opposition Division.[66]

(d) Special considerations concerning maintenance in amended form

3–43   Article 102(3) and Rule 58(4) and (5) EPC contain provisions governing the maintenance of European patents in amended form which are intended to ensure, in particular, that the patent is maintained with a text which has been approved by the proprietor, as required by Article 113(2) EPC.

Article 102(3) and Rule 58(4) EPC do not preclude that an Opposition Division may make an interlocutory decision in respect of a substantive issue before the sending of any Rule 58(4) EPC communication. What is precluded by Rule 58(4) EPC is that the Opposition Division should decide on the maintenance of the European patent in an amended form, without informing the parties of the amended text and inviting observations as there required.

---

[66] T390/86 O.J. EPO 1989, 30.

Article 102(3) EPC also requires in effect that when a patent is maintained in amended form, a new patent specification as to be printed, and to this end, the payment of a printing fee within a prescribed time limit is required, together with translations of any amended claims (Rule 58(5) EPC). These requirements are important in that if they are not complied with, the patent is revoked.

Bearing in mind the possibility of an appeal from a decision of this kind by the Opposition Division, the practice has been to designate this type of decision as interlocutory in the sense of Article 106(3) EPC (see paragraph 4–05 below).[67]

(e) Revocation at the request of the proprietor

If, for whatever reason, the proprietor of a European patent decides **3–44** during opposition proceedings that he no longer wishes to maintain his patent, he may make a request to that effect during the opposition proceedings, and the patent will then be revoked.[68]

(f) Costs

The award of costs in opposition proceedings is discussed in paragraph **3–45** 4–47 below.

(g) Correction of errors in decisions

Rule 89 EPC provides that "only linguistic errors, errors of transcription **3–46** and obvious mistakes [in decisions] may be corrected".

A decision cannot be cancelled by the instance which issued it, but can only be corrected under Rule 89 EPC.[69]

The correction of a mistake in a decision under Rule 89 EPC has a retrospective effect. Any correction of a decision issued by an Opposition Division can only be instigated by the Opposition Division itself (normally by a further decision giving the ground of correction).[70]

K. INTERVENTION IN OPPOSITION PROCEEDINGS BY AN ASSUMED INFRINGER

Article 105 EPC provides a special procedure whereby, after the nine- **3–47** month period under Article 99 EPC for filing an opposition has expired, an alleged infringer may become a party to opposition proceedings, by filing a notice of intervention. The opposition proceedings must be in existence when the notice is filed.[71]

---

[67] G1/88 O.J. EPO 1989, 189.
[68] Legal Advice No. 11/82 O.J. EPO 1982, 57; T73/84 O.J. EPO 1985, 241; T186/84 O.J. EPO 1986, 79; T237/86 O.J. EPO 1988, 261.
[69] T212/88 O.J. EPO 1992, 28.
[70] *Ibid.*
[71] G4/91 O.J. EPO 1993, 77.

(a) Proof required

3–48   In order to be allowed to intervene, the intending intervener must prove either:

    (a) that proceedings for infringement of the European patent have been instituted against him,
    or
    (b) that the patent proprietor has requested that he cease the alleged infringement of the patent, and that he (the intending intervener) has instituted court proceedings for a declaration of non-infringement.

(b) Time limit for filing a notice of intervention

3–49   A notice of intervention must be filed at the EPO within three months from the date on which infringement proceedings (paragraph 3–47 above), or proceedings for a declaration of non-infringement (paragraph 3–48 above), were instituted.

(c) Contents of the notice of intervention

3–50   The notice of intervention must be a "written reasoned statement", and must satisfy the same requirements for admissibility as a notice of opposition (see paragraphs 3–14 *et seq.*, above).

Thereafter the intervention must be "treated as an opposition", except that in accordance with Rule 57(4) EPC, the Opposition Division may dispense with the requirements of Rule 57(1) to (3) EPC (*i.e.* in respect of inviting observations from the proprietor and subsequent replies from the opponents).

(d) Intervention after decision of the Opposition Division

3–51   In a case where, after issue of a final decision by an opposition division, no appeal is filed by a party to the opposition proceedings, a notice of intervention which is filed within the two-month period for appeal provided by Article 108 EPC has no legal effect, because there were no proceedings in existence.[72]

(e) Intervention during appeal proceedings

3–52   Intervention under Article 105 EPC is also possible during pending appeal proceedings following a decision of an Opposition Division, and may be based on any ground for opposition under Article 100 EPC.[73]

L. OBSERVATIONS BY THIRD PARTIES

3–53   The wording of Article 115 EPC provides for the filing of observations in writing concerning the patentability of an invention which is the subject of a granted European patent, when opposition proceedings are pending.

---

[72] *Ibid.*
[73] G1/94 O.J. 1994, 787.

The filing of such observations may be useful in particular if a third party is aware of grounds of objection to a patent which are not known to the EPO, in circumstances where the third party is too late himself to file an opposition.

M. CONCURRENT EPO PROCEEDINGS AND NATIONAL PROCEEDINGS

From the moment when a European patent is granted (*i.e.* from "the 3–54 date on which the European Patent Bulletin mentions the grant" – Article 97(4) EPC) any person may file an opposition at the EPO (within the nine-month period), and revocation proceedings may also be commenced in national courts.

Such opposition proceedings and national revocation proceedings may, therefore, be pending at the same time. The filing of an opposition at the EPO does not suspend the effect of grant of the European patent. The question may then arise whether one or other of these proceedings should be stayed pending completion of the other, in order to avoid duplication, or for other reasons.

The practice concerning staying national proceedings varies in different Contracting States. In the United Kingdom, the Patents Court has refused to stay proceedings before it.[74] In Germany it has been held that pending European grant or opposition proceedings have no prejudicial effect on parallel opposition proceedings before the German Patent Office and cannot constitute grounds for a stay of the national proceedings.[75]

Nevertheless, in other Contracting States it is more common for national proceedings concerning a European patent to be stayed pending the outcome of opposition proceedings before the EPO.

The possibility of concurrent opposition proceedings before the EPO and national proceedings in respect of the validity (and infringement) of the same European patent could lead to the unsatisfactory consequence of conflicting results in the different jurisdictions (*e.g.* a European patent may be held valid in national proceedings but revoked in EPO opposition proceedings, or vice versa).

---

[74] *Amersham International plc v. Corning Ltd* O.J. EPO 1987, 558.
[75] Case No. 4W (pat) 50/85, O.J. EPO 1987, 557.

4. Appeal Procedure

CONTENTS

A. INTRODUCTION

(a) The nature of an appeal

The essential function of an appeal is to consider whether a decision which **4–01**
has been issued by a first instance department is correct on its merits. The
purpose of the appeal procedure in an opposition is mainly to give the losing
party an opportunity to challenge the decision of the Opposition Division on
its merits.[1] The Boards of Appeal are required to give a judicial decision upon
the correctness of the first instance decision under appeal.[2]

Furthermore, in contrast to the administrative character of opposition
proceedings (see paragraph 3–2), the appeal procedure before the Boards
of Appeal is to be considered as a judicial procedure,[3] and is therefore by
its nature less investigative than Opposition Division procedure.

---

[1] G9, 10/91 O.J. EPO 1993, 408 and 420; T26/88 O.J. EPO 1991, 30.
[2] T34/90 O.J. EPO 1992, 454.
[3] G7, 8/91 O.J. EPO 1993, 346 and 356; G9, 10/91 O.J. EPO 1993, 408 and 420.

Thus, as discussed further below (see paragraphs 4–31 to 4–33), the investigative powers of the Boards of Appeal under Article 114(1) EPC are applied more restrictively in an appeal than in proceedings before an Opposition Division.[4]

Appeal proceedings should be considered as wholly separate and independent of the first instance proceedings which are terminated by the decision under appeal, and not merely as a continuation of the first instance proceedings, for all procedural purposes.[5] Thus, any requests of a procedural nature that are made during the first instance proceedings are not automatically applicable in any subsequent appeal proceedings, and have to be made again in the appeal procedure.

The subject matter of appeal proceedings is governed by the appeal which is filed by the appellant.[6]

(b) Stages of appeal procedure

4–02 The EPC provides four general stages of procedure in appeal proceedings before a Board of Appeal:

(a) filing the appeal and examination for admissibility;
(b) substantive examination — written procedure;
(c) substantive examination — optionally including oral proceedings;
(d) making and issuing the decision.

Exceptionally, an additional stage may take place before the decision is made, namely reference of one or more points of law to the Enlarged Board of Appeal (see paragraphs 4–49 to 4–52 below).

The Rules of Procedure of the Boards of Appeal ("RPBA")[7] and of the Enlarged Board of Appeal ("RPEBA")[8] govern the internal operation of the Boards of Appeal and the Enlarged Board of Appeal, and are binding, subject to the EPC.

A brief guide to appeal procedure is contained in a note entitled "Guidance for Appellants and their Representatives,"[9] issued by the Boards of Appeal.

B. FILING AN ADMISSIBLE APPEAL

(a) Filing an appeal

(i) The subject of an appeal—a first instance decision

4–03 An appeal can only be filed in respect of a decision of one of the four first instance departments of the EPO — namely the Receiving Section, the Examining Divisions, the Opposition Divisions, and the Legal Division

---

[4] *Ibid.*
[5] T34/90 O.J. EPO 1992, 454.
[6] G9/92, G4/93 O.J. EPO 1994, 875.
[7] O.J. EPO 1989, 361.
[8] O.J. EPO 1989, 362.
[9] O.J. EPO 1989, 395.

(Article 106(1) EPC). The Boards of Appeal are responsible for the examination of appeals from such first instance departments (Article 21(1) EPC).

(ii) Formal contents of a first instance decision

A decision may be issued orally during proceedings, or in writing. If **4–04** given orally, the decision in writing shall be notified to the parties (Rule 68(1) EPC). All decisions which are open to appeal must be reasoned.

All first instance decisions are thus required to consist of two essential parts — a statement as to what has been decided, and a statement of the reasons for what has been decided. When a substantive decision is given orally during oral proceedings, such substantive decisions must be formally completed by the giving of reasons for the decision in writing.[10]

In practice, all written decisions normally consist of a "Summary of Facts and Submissions" and "Reasons for the Decision," ending with a statement of what has been decided (the "order").

Rule 68(2) EPC requires every decision to be accompanied by a "written communication of the possibility of appeal," with the text of Articles 106 to 108 EPC attached. However, the omission of such a communication may not be invoked by the parties, and such omission does not by itself invalidate the decision if the other requirements of a decision are satisfied.

(iii) Interlocutory decisions — separate appeal allowable

Article 106(3) EPC provides that "A decision which does not terminate **4–05** proceedings as regards one of the parties can only be appealed together with the final decision, unless the decision allows separate appeal."

This provision is particularly important connection with decisions pursuant to Article 102(3) EPC, in which the Opposition Division decides to maintain patent in amended form. In such cases, a separate appeal is in practice allowed.

An Opposition Division may give interlocutory decisions on substantive issues during the course of the proceedings and such decisions may be separately appealable (*e.g.* on the allowability of a proposed amendment).[11]

(iv) Decision compared with mere intention to decide

It is necessary to distinguish between a decision of a first instance **4–06** department and a mere intention to decide. The importance of this distinction arises particularly in examination proceedings under Article 97(2) and Rule 51(4) EPC and in opposition proceedings under Article 102(3) and Rule 58(4) EPC. In examination proceedings, if an Examining Division decides to grant a patent, before actually issuing such a decision it

---

[10] T390/86 O.J. EPO 1989, 30.
[11] *Ibid.*

must first establish that the applicant approves the text of the patent. It does this by issuing a communication under Rule 51(4) EPC which informs the applicant of the text in which it intends to grant it (see paragraph 2–26). Similarly, in opposition proceedings, if an Opposition Division decides to maintain the grant of a patent in amended form, before issuing such a decision it must first establish that the patentee approves the amended form of the text, by issuing a communication under Rule 58(4) EPC (see paragraph 3–42). Such communications under Rule 51(4) and Rule 58(4) EPC always indicate an intention to decide the matters in issue, and are not decisions as such.

(v) Decisions, communications and notifications distinguished

4–07   The EPC distinguishes between decisions, communications and notices or notifications issued by first instance departments (see, e.g. Rule 70 EPC).

A decision decides one or more issues. A communication normally invites observations in reply. A notification normally gives notice of some event, without inviting observations in reply.

During first instance procedure before the EPO, especially during examination and opposition proceedings, there are many occasions when a "communication" is sent to a party to the proceedings, and such a communication commonly expresses a point of view which is adverse to a party, and invites observations in reply. Such a communication is never binding upon the department of the EPO which issued it, and cannot be the subject of an appeal.

Similarly, there are many occasions during first instance proceedings when notifications are issued to parties, under Article 119 EPC (and see Rules 69 and 77 to 82 EPC). Such notifications must also be clearly distinguished from decisions which are subject to appeal.

While the above mentioned classes of documents should normally be clearly identified as such, the title of such a document (or lack of it) is not necessarily decisive as to its true nature.

Whether a document constitutes a decision (within the meaning of Article 106(1) EPC) depends on the substance of its contents, not upon its form,[12] and depends also upon its context within the proceedings in which it was issued.

(vi) No decision within Article 106(1) EPC

4–08   If an appeal is filed against a document which purports to be a decision, or which is thought to be a decision, within the meaning of Article 106(1) EPC, the Board of Appeal will examine the appeal both for admissibility and, if appropriate, for allowability.

If the Board of Appeal decides that the document is not a decision within the meaning of Article 106(1) EPC, but is merely a communication

---

[12] J8/81 O.J. EPO 1982, 10.

or notification on its proper interpretation, the appeal is held to be inadmissible, on the basis that there can be no appeal from a non-existent decision.

(b) Parties to an appeal

(i) The appellant

An appeal may be filed — and may only be filed — by a party to **4–09** proceedings before one of the four first instance departments of the EPO who is "adversely affected" by a decision of such first instance department (Article 107 EPC). A party who is adversely affected by such a decision has a right to appeal — no leave to appeal is required.

(ii) Meaning of "adversely affected"

A party can only be adversely affected by a decision when such a **4–10** decision is inconsistent with what he has specifically requested.[13]

For example, an applicant is adversely affected by a decision to grant a patent with a text which was not approved by the applicant in accordance with Article 91(2)(a) and Rule 51(4) EPC.[14]

Under Article 106(1) EPC appeals lie from decisions rather than from the grounds of such decisions.[15] Thus, a party to opposition proceedings is not adversely affected by a decision which corresponds to what he has requested, even if the reasoning for such decision is contrary to his contentions. For example, if the claims of a granted patent are held to be novel and are therefore maintained as granted and as requested by the patentee, but in the reasoning of the decision such claims are held not to be entitled to the claimed priority date, the patentee is not "adversely affected" by such reasoning within the meaning of Article 107 EPC.[16]

(iii) Multiple appeals

More than one party to opposition proceedings may be adversely **4–11** affected by a decision. For example, if a patent is maintained in amended form in accordance with an auxiliary request (see paragraphs 3–29 and 3–40 above), the patentee is adversely affected by the decision not to maintain the patent as granted, and the opponent is adversely by the decision not to revoke the patent. In such a case both the patentee and the opponent may file an appeal.

Similarly, in any opposition by several opponents in which the patent is maintained, each unsuccessful opponent is adversely affected by such a decision and therefore has a right to appeal.

The filing of an appeal by an adversely affected party to opposition proceedings gives that party the right to continue the appeal proceedings

---

[13] J12/85 O.J. EPO 1986, 155.
[14] J12/83 O.J. EPO 1985, 6.
[15] T611/90 O.J. EPO 1993, 50.
[16] T73/88 O.J. EPO 1992, 557.

even if other appeals are withdrawn (as to withdrawal of an appeal, see paragraph 4–36 below). Conversely, such an adversely affected party to opposition proceedings who does not file an appeal may not continue the appeal proceedings if the other appeals are withdrawn.[17]

(iv) Other parties to an appeal: respondents and parties as of right

4–12   Article 107 EPC, provides that: "Any other parties to the [first instance] proceedings shall be parties to the appeal proceedings as of right." In an opposition by only one opponent, a party who is adversely affected by the decision of the Opposition Division may appeal, and the other party is then the respondent if he does not file an appeal. In an opposition by several opponents who are all unsuccessful and therefore adversely affected, if one such unsuccessful opponent appeals, both the patentee and the other opponents are parties to the appeal proceedings as of right.

(v) Effect of failure to appeal by an adversely affected party

4–13   An adversely affected party to opposition proceedings who does not file an appeal may not contend in appeal proceedings commenced by another party that the contested decision was wrong. As a respondent he may argue in support of such decision. A request by a party to appeal proceedings who has not filed an appeal which goes beyond the appellant's appeal request is inadmissible.

Thus, as adversely affected opponent who does not file an appeal may not contend in appeal proceedings commenced by the patentee that the patent should be revoked. An adversely affected patentee who does not file an appeal is primarily restricted during appeal proceedings commenced by the opponent to defending the patent as maintained by the Opposition Division.[18] As to the filing of amendments by the patentee in such a case, see paragraph 4–30 below.

(c) Formal requirements for filing an appeal

(i) Time limits

4–14   A decision of a first instance department is sent to the parties by registered post with advice of delivery — Rule 78(1) EPC. Notification of the decision is deemed to take place in all cases on the 10th day following its posting (*i.e.* even if it was in fact received earlier than the 10th day), unless the registered letter fails to arrive or arrives after the 10th day — Rule 78(3) EPC. In the event of any dispute as to notification, the burden of proof lies on the EPO "to establish that the letter has reached its destination or to establish the date on which the letter was delivered to the addressee, as the case may be." (Rule 78(3) EPC).

---

[17] G2/91 O.J. EPO 1992, 206; G7, 8/91, O.J. EPO 1993, 346 and 356.
[18] G9/92, G4/93 O.J. EPO 1994, 875.

A notice of appeal must be filed, and the appeal fee paid, within two months after the date of notification of the decision under appeal (Article 108 EPC). The notice of appeal is deemed not to have been filed until the appeal fee is paid.

The two-month period is calculated in accordance with Rule 83(2) EPC by reference to the date of notification determined as above. Under this Rule the two-month period commences the day after the date of notification. Thus, for example, if a decision is issued on March 1, and is received by a party within 10 days, the date of notification is deemed to be March 11, and a notice of appeal must be filed by May 11 (subject to Rule 85(1) EPC).

Similarly, a statement of grounds of appeal must be filed within four months after the date of notification of the decision, calculated in the same way.

(ii) Beginning of the time limits

Article 108 EPC does not forbid the filing of an appeal before **4–15** notification of the decision, but merely prescribes that it cannot be filed later than two months after this notification. Thus, a notice of appeal may be filed before the date of notification of a decision.[19]

(iii) Notice of appeal

The essential contents of a notice of appeal are set out in Rule 64 EPC **4–16** as follows:

(a) the name and address of the appellant (see Rule 26(2)(c) EPC);
(b) a statement identifying:
    (i) the decision which is impugned, and
    (ii) the extent to which amendment or cancellation of the decision is
        requested.

The purpose of requirement (a) is to identify the appellant and his address, in order that postal correspondence with him can take place. In the event of non-compliance with this requirement within the two-month time limit of Article 108 EPC, under Rule 65(2) EPC the Board of Appeal is required to invite the appellant to remedy the deficiencies within a specified period. Only after continued non-compliance beyond such specified period may the Board reject the appeal as inadmissible.

The purpose of requirement (b)(i) is to identify the decision which is to be challenged. It is necessary to be able to identify this within the two-month time limit for appeal under Article 108 EPC, in order that the date of notification of the decision can be determined and the expiry date of the two-month period calculated. Thus, if the decision which is impugned is not sufficiently identified, under Rule 65(1) EPC the Board will reject the appeal as inadmissible unless the deficiency is rectified within the two-

---

[19] T389/86 O.J. EPO 1988, 87.

month appeal period. Rectification in this situation would seem to require sufficient identification at least for the calculation of the two-month period.

As to requirement (b)(ii), in the absence of such a statement of "the extent to which amendment or cancellation of the decision is requested" in the notice of appeal, such a notice of appeal may be interpreted as being against the entire contents of the first instance decision which is impugned[20] (especially when it is clear by implication what is being sought). On a strict view of this requirement in Rule 64(b) EPC, however, a notice of appeal could be considered inadmissible in the absence of an express statement.

When drafting a notice of appeal, it is clearly desirable to ensure that all the requirements of Rule 64 EPC are specifically compiled with, in order to avoid any risk of rejection of the appeal on the ground of inadmissibility.

(iv) Language

4–17   An appeal may be filed in any official language of the EPO (English, French or German) — Rule 1(1) EPC. This is subject to Articles 14(2) and (4) EPC, which together provide that "natural or legal person having their residenc or principal place of business" within a Contracting State having a language other than English, French or German as an official language (*e.g.* Holland) may file documents which have to be filed within a time limit (such as a notice of appeal) in an official language of the Contracting State concerned (*e.g.* Dutch). However, a translation into one of the three official languages of the EPO must then be filed with a prescribed period (Rule 6(2) EPC) although it may accompany the notice of appeal.[21] If no such translation is filed in due time, the appeal is not brought into existence[22] and the appeal fee is therefore refunded.[23]

A 20 percent reduction in the appeal fee is provided by Rule 6(3) EPC to an appellant who files a notice of appeal in such a language. It is not necessary to file the statement of grounds of appeal in such a language in order to obtain the fee reduction.[24]

(v) Existence of an appeal

4–18   As noted above, under Article 108 EPC a notice of appeal "shall not be deemed to have been filed until after the fee for appeal has been paid," — even if the notice of appeal has in fact been filed before the appeal fee is paid.

However, if a notice of appeal has been filed and the appeal fee has been paid within the two-month appeal period of Article 108 EPC, an appeal is

---

[20] *e.g.* T7/81 O.J. EPO 1983, 98.
[21] G6/91 O.J. EPO 1992, 491.
[22] T323/87 O.J. EPO 1989, 343.
[23] *Ibid.*
[24] G6/91 O.J. EPO 1992, 491.

thereby brought into existence. Thereafter, a refund of the appeal fee cannot be obtained by withdrawing the appeal[25] or by failing to file a statement of grounds of appeal.[26]

If the notice of appeal is physically filed within the two-month period, but the appeal fee is not paid in due time but is paid late, it is refunded because no appeal is brought into existence.[27]

It is possible that if an appeal fee is paid in due time, but the notice of appeal is filed outside the two-month period, the appeal fee would be refunded on the basis that an appeal did not come into existence.[28]

(vi) Suspensive effect of an appeal

Article 106(1) EPC provides that an appeal has "suspensive effect." This **4–19** means that the consequences of the decision under appeal (*e.g.* revocation of a patent) do not ensue so long as the appeal is pending.

(vii) The statement of grounds of appeal: substantive contents

Contesting the decision under appeal. In contrast to the essential con- **4–20** tents of a notice of appeal, which are specified in Rule 64 EPC, Article 108 EPC does not specify the essential contents of the statement of grounds of appeal but merely prescribes that "a written statement setting out the grounds of appeal must be filed" (within the four months period).

While the filing of such a statement within the prescribed time limit is a formal requirement, the contents of such a statement have to be substantive in nature. Article 108 EPC provides an additional two months, beyond the two-month period prescribed for filing a notice of appeal, during which the grounds of appeal must be filed, and thus clearly envisages that the grounds of appeal should contain something more than what is required to be included in the notice of appeal.

The statement of grounds of appeal should contain a presentation of the appellant's case including the substance of the appellant's case: that is, the reasons why the appeal should be allowed and why the decision under appeal should be set aside. A well-drafted statement of grounds should contain reasoning that is full but concise. The less reasoning that a statement contains the greater will be the risk that the appeal will be rejected as inadmissible.[29]

Thus, the grounds of appeal should state the legal and factual reasons why the decision under appeal should be set aside and the appeal allowed.[30] It is not enought merely to assert that the decision under appeal is wrong, even if the same issues arise in the appeal.[31]

---

[25] T41/82 O.J. EPO 1982, 256.
[26] *e.g.* T13/82 O.J. EPO 1983, 411.
[27] J21/80 O.J. EPO 1981, 101.
[28] *e.g.* T13/82 O.J. EPO 1983, 411.
[29] J22/86 O.J. EPO 1987, 280.
[30] T145/88 O.J. EPO 1991, 251.
[31] *e.g.* T432/88 [1990] EPOR 38.

Furthermore, in a case concerning inventive step, it is not sufficient for the appellants merely to refer in general terms to passages from the literature showing the state of the art and to the *Guidelines for Examination in the EPO* without making their inferences adequately clear.[32]

It is, of course, important that the grounds of appeal should deal with the actual grounds on which the decision under appeal is based. Thus, in one case an opposition was rejected as inadmissible by the Opposition Division, on the basis that the notice of opposition contained insufficient support for the ground of opposition alleged. What should have been in issue on appeal, therefore, was the admissibility of the notice of opposition. The grounds of appeal did not deal with this issue, but merely attempted to supplement the ground of opposition; and the appeal was accordingly held to be inadmissible as well.[33]

An appeal which raises a fresh case which is entirely different from that on which the decision under appeal was based is admissible if it is based upon the same ground of opposition.[34]

It is normally necessary to state specific reasons why the decision is wrong, either in its statements of the facts or in its application of the law, or both.

Nevertheless, whether a particular statement alleged to be a statement of grounds of appeal in a particular case meets the requirements of Article 108 EPC can only be decided in the context of that particular case; and the content of a particular case will normally include the contents of the decision under appeal.[35]

In general, the same broad principles are applicable to the admissibility of a statement of grounds of appeal as are applicable to a notice of opposition.

Change of circumstances since decision under appeal. In a particular class of appeal cases, the circumstances of the case change between issue of the first instance decision and the time when the grounds of appeal are filed. This commonly occurs when an appellant in effect admits that the adverse first instance decision was correct for the claims on which the decision was based, but submits a proposed amended set of claims for consideration in the appeal (*e.g.* in the statement of grounds of appeal).

Generally, grounds of appeal will satisfy the requirements of Article 108 EPC if they refer to a new circumstance which, if confirmed, will invalidate the contested decision.[36]

(d) Examination for admissibility

4–21   Rule 65 EPC prescribes that a Board of Appeal shall reject an appeal as inadmissible if the requirements of Articles 106 to 108 and Rule 64 EPC are not complied with. These requirements have been discussed above.

---

[32] T220/83 O.J. EPO 1986, 249.
[33] T213/85 O.J. EPO 1987, 482.
[34] T611/90 O.J. EPO 1993, 50.
[35] J22/86 O.J. EPO 1987, 280.
[36] J22/86 O.J. EPO 1987, 280.

The purpose of the examination for admissibility is to determine whether the appeal may go forward for substantive examination and decision. Unless an appeal is admissible, the Board of Appeal may not examine whether the appeal is allowable (Article 110(1) EPC).

(e) Interlocutory revision

Under Article 109(1) EPC, the notice of appeal and the statement of **4–22** grounds of appeal are initially considered by the first instance department whose decision is impugned. If that department "considers the appeal to be admissible and well founded, it shall rectify its decision." Thus, an opportunity is provided for a first instance department to have second thoughts on its decision, after having seen the grounds of appeal. There is therefore a strong incentive in appropriate cases to set out as clearly as possible in the statement of grounds of appeal the legal and factual reasons why the decision under appeal should be set aside.

Interlocutory revision is not possible in proceedings where the appellant is opposed by another party (Article 109(1) EPC, second sentence).

Rule 67 EPC provides that in the event of interlocutory revision, reimbursement of the appeal fee shall be ordered if appropriate by the first instance department which gave the decision under appeal.

Article 109(2) EPC provides that "if the appeal is not allowed within one month after receipt of the statement of grounds, it shall be remitted to the Board of Appeal without delay, and without comment as to its merit." While the relatively short period of one month is understandable in order to avoid a prolonged re-examination and consequent delay, it also serves to prevent much use being made of the provision.

(i) A "well founded" appeal

(1) An appeal is clearly well-founded if, upon examination of the **4–23** statement of grounds of appeal, the first instance department itself recognises that the decision under appeal should not after all be supported, on its merits; in other words, when the first instance department is persuaded by the grounds of appeal or otherwise is prepared to set aside its own previous decision.

(2) An appeal is also to be considered well-founded if the amendments submitted by the appellant clearly meet the objections on which the decision under appeal relies. The existence of other objections which have not been removed but which were not the subject of such decision do not preclude the application of Article 109 EPC.[37]

(3) An appeal may also be considered as well-founded if the appellant no longer seeks grant of the patent with a text corresponding to that which was rejected by the Examining Division, and if substantial amendments are proposed which are clearly intended to overcome the objections raised in the decision under appeal. Rectification of

---

[37] T139/87 O.J. EPO 1990, 69.

the previous decision does not preclude a further adverse decision in respect of the amended text.[38]

In this context substantial amendments are those which require a substantial further examination in relation to the requirements of the EPC.[39]

Thus, where the amendments proposed to the text of the patent by the main request in the appeal are sufficiently substantial for a Board of Appeal to remit the case to the first instance under Article 111(1) EPC, they are also in principle sufficiently substantial for the first instance department to rectify its own decision which is under appeal by way of interlocutory revision. In either case, the consequent further examination of the case by the Examining Division may lead to a further decision which may or may not be favourable to the appellant.

Interlocutory revision in these circumstances means that in the event of another adverse decision by the first instance department, the appellant again has the right to appeal, thus preserving the possibility of consideration of the merits of the case by two instances.

(ii) Failure to apply interlocutory revision

4–24   Normally, if the Examining Division does not rectify its decision by way of interlocutory revision, an applicant has no remedy, even if he has specifically requested this in the grounds of appeal. In the absence of interlocutory revision, the Board of Appeal may still remit the case to the Examining Division (see paragraph 4—34 below).

In certain circumstances, however, a failure to apply interlocutory revision can amount to a substantial procedural violation justifying refund of the appeal fee (see paragraph 4–48 below).

C. SUBSTANTIVE EXAMINATION OF AN APPEAL

(a) Introduction

(i) General characteristics

4–25   Following due filing of the notice of appeal and the statement of grounds of appeal, the consideration in respect of interlocutory revision under Article 109 EPC, and the examination for admissibility under Rule 65 EPC, an appeal is ready for substantive examination and decision under Articles 110 and 111 and Rule 66 EPC.

There are two basic categories of appeal proceedings—*ex parte* proceedings and *inter partes* (*i.e.* opposition) proceedings, which will be considered separately where necessary. The procedure in appeals from decisions of the Examining Division and the Opposition Division is similar to the

---

[38] T47/90 O.J. EPO 1991, 486.
[39] T63/86 O.J. EPO 1988, 224.

respective procedures before those departments themselves (see Rule 66(1) EPC).

Oral proceedings are optional either at the request of a party or at the instance of the Board of Appeal (see paragraph 4–38 below). The procedure is therefore necessarily arranged so as to provide for clarification of the issues in the appeal as far as possible in writing, prior to the making of a decision in the case. Such clarification of the issues in writing has the advantages of sometimes avoiding the need for oral proceedings which might otherwise be required, and if there are oral proceedings, helping to keep these reasonably short. This is expecially desirable having regard to the international nature of many of the cases, and the consequent need for parties and their representatives sometimes to travel a considerable distance in order to attend oral proceedings.

The prior clarification of the issues in writing normally enables the decision to be made and announced at the conclusion of the oral proceedings.

In practice, less than half the appeals filed are currently decided without any oral proceedings and therefore solely on the written documents in the case. Opposition proceedings commonly include oral proceedings.

(ii) Characteristics of the written examination stage

It is the written examination stage of an appeal, governed by Article 110 **4–26** and Rule 66(1) EPC, which gives the appeal procedure under the EPC its most distinctive characteristics, which are:

(a) the work of the "rapporteur", the member of the Board who initially studies an appeal (see Article 4 (RPBA);
(b) the flexibility of the procedure;
(c) the control of the procedure by the Board.

(iii) Similarity of procedure in first instance and appeal proceedings

The majority of cases before the Boards of Appeal are appeals from **4–27** decisions of the Examining Division and the Opposition Division, and are therefore examined and decided by Technical Boards of Appeal (Article 21 EPC).

Rule 66(1) EPC states that "Unless otherwise provided, the provisions relating to procedure before the department from which the appeal is brought shall be applicable to appeal proceedings mutatis mutandis." In addition, Article 111(1) EPC provides, in the context of deciding on an appeal, that "The Board of Appeal may . . . exercise any power within the competence of the (first instance) department which was responsible for the decision appealed . . .". Alternatively, under Article 111(1) EPC, a Board of Appeal may remit a case to that first instance department (see paragraph 4–34).

(b) Procedure during the written examination stage

Substantive examination of an appeal by a Board of Appeal begins when **4–28** the initial submissions by the parties are complete. In *ex parte* proceedings, these are the notice of appeal and the statement of grounds of appeal. In *inter partes* proceedings, the respondent is always invited to file observations upon the grounds of appeal.

(i) Communications and observations in reply

4–29 **Ex parte proceedings.** If, after consideration of the grounds of appeal, the Board intends to allow the appeal, no communication on behalf of the Board is necessary, and a decision favourable to the appellant may be issued directly.

If, after such consideration, the Board is not able to issue a favourable decision directly, two kinds of communication are possible:

—A communication under Article 110(2) EPC. Grounds of objection to grant are normally contained in such a communication, and it is then necessary to invite observations in reply within a fixed period of time, normally two to four months (which may be extended on application).

A reply to such a communication must be filed in due time. Article 110(3) EPC provides that if the applicant fails to reply in due time to an invitation under Article 110(2) EPC, "the application shall be deemed to be withdrawn."

This provision does not apply to an appeal from a decision of the Legal Division (Article 110(3) EPC). Nor does it apply in opposition proceedings.

—A communication in preparation for oral proceedings under Article 11(2) RPBA. If oral proceedings have been requested, a communication may be sent in preparation for such proceedings, accompanied by the summons to oral proceedings. In this case, there is no specific invitation to file observations in reply, either within a fixed period or at all. Nevertheless, in advance of oral proceedings the appellant may make submissions in writing by a date which is fixed in the communication. New facts and evidence presented after that date need not be considered, unless admitted on the ground that the subject of the proceedings has changed (Rule 71a EPC — in force from June 1, 1995). The appellant's comments upon the Board's communication may be made at the oral hearing itself.

Inter partes proceedings. Where no request for oral proceedings has been made, a Board will send a communication to the parties to ensure compliance with Article 113(1) EPC, namely to give the parties an opportunity to comment upon the grounds and evidence upon which the decision may eventually be based.

Where oral proceedings have been requested, the Board may send with the summons to oral proceedings a communication drawing attention to matters which seem to be of special significance, or to the fact that questions appear no longer to be contentious, or containing other observations that may help concentration on essentials during the oral proceedings (Article 11(2) RPBA). Such communication shall fix a date by which written submissions may be filed. As in *ex parte* proceedings, new facts and evidence filed after that date need not be considered, except if the subject of the proceedings has changed (Rule 71a EPC — in force from June 1, 1995).

(ii) Amendments in appeal proceedings

Following refusal of an application or revocation of a patent by the first **4–30** instance, newly formulated claims are commonly presented in the course of subsequent appeal proceedings commenced by the patentee, normally, with the statement of grounds of appeal.

The submission of amendments is generally regulated by Article 123 and Rule 86(3) EPC. Rule 86(3) EPC applies in appeal proceedings because of Rule 66(1) EPC. If it is desired to submit amendments to the description, claims or drawings of a patent application during appeal proceedings, this should be done at the earliest possible moment. The Board concerned may, for example, disregard amendments which, when the applicant has been invited to file observations, are submitted after the time for answering the invitation has expired or, when a date for oral proceedings has been given, are not submitted in good time before the proceedings.[40]

The practice of filing main and auxiliary requests which is followed in the first instance procedure (see paragraphs 2–15 and 3–29) also applies in appeal proceedings. An applicant or patentee should ensure that any auxiliary requests are filed as early as possible during appeal proceedings.

If a patent is maintained in amended form by the Opposition Division, and an opponent appeals and requests revocation of the patent, the patentee is primarily restricted during the appeal proceedings to defending the patent as so maintained. Amendments proposed by the patentee as a "party as of right" to the appeal proceedings (see paragraphs 4–12 and 4–13 above) may be held inadmissible if they do not arise out of the opponent's appeal.[41]

(iii) Late-filed amendments

Proposed amendments to the claims filed at a late state in appeal **4–31** proceedings, whether *ex parte* or *inter partes*, may be refused if they are not clearly allowable.

The normal rule is as follows: if an appellant wishes that the allowability of an alternative set of claims, which differ in subject matter from those considered at first instance, should be considered by the Board of Appeal when deciding on the appeal, such alternative sets of claims should be filed with the grounds of appeal, or as soon as possible thereafter.

It is only in the most exceptional circumstances, where there is some clear justification both for the amendment and for its late submission, that it is likely that an amendment not submitted in good time before oral

---

[40] "Guidance for Appellants and their Representatives," O.J. EPO 1989, 395.
[41] G9/92, G4/93 O.J. EPO 1994, 875.

proceedings will be considered on its merits in those proceedings by a Board of Appeal. When deciding on an appeal during oral proceedings, a Bord may justifiably refuse to consider alternative claims which have been filed at a very late stage, for example during the oral proceedings, if such alternative claims are not clearly allowable.[42]

(iv) Late-filed additional grounds of opposition during opposition appeals

4–32 In principle, fresh grounds of opposition cannot be introduced into appeal proceedings. However, an exception to the above principle is justified if the patentee agrees that such a fresh ground may be considered, and if such fresh ground is considered by the Board of Appeal to be highly relevant.

If the patentee does not agree to the introduction of a fresh ground of opposition, such ground may not be dealt with in the decision at all.[43]

(v) Late-filed documents and evidence in support

4–33 Late-filed documents, facts or evidence in support of grounds of opposition may be admitted into appeal proceedings by a Board of Appeal in the exercise of its discretion under Article 114(1) EPC, depending particularly upon its relevance to such grounds.[44] After the admission of such a document into the proceedings, it is then a matter of further discretion for the Board of Appeal under Article 111(1) EPC whether the case should be remitted to the Opposition Division or whether the Board should itself consider and decide upon the case including the new document (see paragraph 4–34 below). As to the award of costs in such circumstances, see paragraph 4–47 below.

New facts, evidence and related arguments which go beyond the "indication of facts, evidence and arguments" presented in the notice of opposition pursuant to Rule 55(c) EPC (see paragraph 3–18 above) in support of the grounds on which the opposition is based should only very exceptionally be admitted into the proceedings, if such new material is prima facie highly relevant in the sense that it can reasonably be expected to change the eventual result and is thus highly likely to prejudice the maintenance of the opposed patent. The Board of Appeal may also take account of other relevant factors, in particular whether the patent proprietor objects to the new material being admitted and the reasons for any such objection, and the degree of procedural complication that its admission is likely to cause.

Thus, the admissibility of such new material before the Boards of Appeal is more restricted than before the Opposition Division (cf. paragraph 3–32 above), having regard to the judicial nature of appeal

---

[42] T95/83 O.J. EPO 1985, 75; T153/85 O.J. EPO 1988, 1.
[43] G9, 10/91 O.J. EPO 1993, 408 and 420.
[44] T271/84 O.J. EPO 1987, 405; T142/84 O.J. EPO 1987, 112; T156/84 O.J. EPO 1988, 372.

proceedings and the fact that an opponent has the opportunity to bring subsequent revocation proceedings based on such new material before national courts (see paragraph 1–04 above and 3–54 below).

In the event of an abuse of procedure by a party (for example, withholding evidence of prior use based upon an opponent's own activities until a late stage in the proceeding without good reason), or in the absence of adequate excuse for its lateness, late-filed facts and evidence may be disregarded under Article 114(2) EPC irrespective of its relevance.[45]

(vi) Remittal to the first instance

Under Article 111(1) EPC, following initial examination of an appeal, **4–34** the Board of Appeal has the power to remit the case to the first instance for further prosecution. There are a number of particular circumstances where this power has been exercised in order to ensure that points may be examined and decided by two instances:

Following amendment of claims. When amended claims are filed during appeal proceedings, either with the grounds of appeal or at a later stage, which are intended to replace the claims which were refused by the first instance, the Board of Appeal has to exercise its discretion under Article 111(1) EPC, either to decide upon the allowability of the new claims, or to remit the case to the first instance.

One major factor in the exercise of this discretion must be the substantiality of the proposed amendments. Minor amendments, primarily of a clarifying nature for example, which do not affect the basis on which the decision under appeal was made, clearly do not justify remittal to the first instance. On the other hand, substantial amendments to the claims constituting the main request of the appellant may justify such remittal.[46]

Another major factor in the exercise of this discretion is the stage at which the amendments are proposed. The later the amendments are proposed in appeal proceedings, and the more involved the Board of Appeal is in the case, the less likely it is that remittal will be ordered.

Following introduction of a fresh ground of opposition. If a fresh ground of opposition is admitted into appeal proceedings, the case should be remitted to the first instance for further prosecution, unless special reasons are present.[47]

Following introduction of new documents or evidence in support. If a new document is admitted which changes the nature of the case, the case should normally be remitted to the first instance.[48] An award of costs may then be justified. If the patentee does not want the case to be remitted, the Board of Appeal may continue to examine and decide the case itself.[49]

---

[45] T1002/92 O.J. EPO (P), T534/89 O.J. EPO 1994, 464, T951/91 O.J. EPO (P).
[46] T63/86 O.J. EPO 1988, 224.
[47] G9, 10/91 O.J. EPO 1993, 408 and 420.
[48] T273/84 O.J. EPO 1986, 346; T326/87 O.J. EPO 1992, 522.
[49] T258/84 O.J. EPO 1987, 119.

A decision upon issues not previously considered. It frequently happens that a first instance department issues a decision upon one particular issue which is decisive for the case against a party, and leaves other issues outstanding. If, following appeal proceedings, the appeal on the particular issue is allowed, the case is normally remitted to the first instance department for consideration of the undecided issues, or of issues not properly considered by the first instance.[50]

White the appropriateness of such a course by a first instance department is a matter of discretion in each case, where practicable it is clearly desirable to avoid the necessity for remittal, in order to bring the overall proceedings to a close as soon as reasonably possible.

(c) Completion of the written examination stage

4–35   The examination stage under Article 111 EPC is completed when the parties have filed their observations on communications from the Board of Appeal or other parties (or when the time limit for filing such observations has expired). The rapporteur (see paragraph 4–26 above) will then consult with the other members of the Board as to the further procedure. If there has been no request for oral proceedings, either a communication may be issued or the written decision may be drafted and issued. Alternatively, if oral proceedings have been requested, a summons to oral proceedings may be issued (with or without an accompanying communication under Article 11(2) RPBA).

(d) Effect of withdrawal of an appeal

4–36   In general, an appeal pending before a Board of Appeal of the EPO can be withdrawn without the consent of the Board concerned. Part of an appeal can be withdrawn in a case in which the part in question relates to a specific issue which formed a distinct part of the decision.[51]

If there is more than one appellant, in the event of withdrawal by one appellant, the appeal(s) by the other appellant(s) are continued.

If only one appeal is filed, the withdrawal of the appeal immediately and automatically terminates the appeal proceedings, and the decision under appeal becomes immediately effective.[52]

If an opponent/appellant states during appeal proceedings that "the opposition" is withdrawn, this is considered as equivalent to withdrawal of the appeal, with consequences as set out above.[52a]

(e) Accelerated processing of an appeal

4–37   Depending upon the circumstances of a case, a Board of Appeal has a discretion to examine a particular appeal out of turn and thus to accelerate the processing of and decision in respect of that appeal.

---

[50] T19/90 O.J. EPO 1990, 476.
[51] J19/82 O.J. EPO 1984, 6.
[52] G7, 8/91 O.J. EPO 1993, 346 and 356.
[52a] G8/93 O.J. EPO 1994, 887.

If infringement proceedings in a designated State have been commenced or are contemplated by the patentee, it is justifiable to give priority to an appeal in opposition proceedings and to decide it in advance of other pending appeals.[53]

D. ORAL PROCEEDINGS

(a) Introduction: when appointed

Oral proceedings before a first instance department or a Board of Appeal do not take place in every case automatically, but may take place either following a decision to that effect by the EPO, or following a request from a party to proceedings before the EPO.

4–38

(i) Appointment by the EPO

Article 116(1) EPC provides that oral proceedings shall take place "at the instance of the EPO if it considers this to be expedient." However, as a matter of practice, it is rare for oral proceedings to be appointed either by a first instance department or by a Board of Appeal of its own motion and in the absence of a request from a party.

(ii) Appointment upon request by a party

Generally, a party to proceedings before any department or instance of the EPO has a right to oral proceedings under Article 116 EPC upon request. This right to an oral hearing is subject to two exceptions:

Second or further requests. If an oral hearing has already taken place in proceedings before a department of the EPO then, according to the second sentence of Article 116(1) EPC, "the EPO may reject a request for further oral proceedings before the same department where the parties and the subject of the proceedings are the same."

Proceedings before the Receiving Section. The appointment of an oral hearing during proceedings before the Receiving Section is always discretionary,[54] except when a refusal of a patent application is envisaged—Article 116(2) EPC.

(iii) The right to oral proceedings upon request

Subject to Article 116(2) EPC, it is clear from the mandatory wording of Article 116(1) EPC that a party who requests oral proceedings is entitled to such proceedings once as of right.[55] If, on the proper interpretation of a

---

[53] T290/90 O.J. EPO 1992, 368.
[54] See *e.g.* Decision without number, O.J. EPO 1985, 159; J20/87 O.J. EPO 1989, 67.
[55] See, *e.g.* T299/86 O.J. EPO 1988, 88; T19/87 O.J. EPO 1988, 268.

communication from a party, it contains a request for oral proceedings, there is no power to issue an adverse decision without first appointing oral proceedings. If an adverse decision is issued in such circumstances, it is void.

In practice, Article 116(1) EPC is interpreted as being applicable only so as to give a party a right to oral proceedings if it is intended or envisaged that a decision may be issued which is adverse to that party. Most requests for oral proceedings are made in that sense (for example, "on an auxiliary basis").

(b) Requesting oral proceedings

4–39   Under Article 116 EPC, a party is entitled to make a request for oral proceedings at any time during the course of proceedings before a particular department or Board of Appeal. A fresh request has to be filed in the event of an appeal, since this constitutes new proceedings.[56]

If there is a possibility that oral proceedings will be desired in particular proceedings, a party should make such a request at the start of or at an early stage in the proceedings, since such a request can always subsequently be withdrawn.

The right of a party to have oral proceedings is dependent upon such party filing a request for such proceedings: in the absence of such a request, a party has no right to such proceedings, and the EPO can issue a decision, whether adverse or not, without appointing such proceedings.[57]

If oral proceedings are required, it is essential that the form of the request should be clear. The need for clarity is especially necessary if misunderstandings are to be avoided, bearing in mind the multinational membership of the EPO.

If there is any doubt in a particular case as to whether or not oral proceedings have been requested, clarification is normally sought from the party concerned.

In some cases, requests for interviews have become confused with requests for oral proceedings. Oral proceedings must be clearly distinguished from interviews. The practice in relation to the holding of interviews is clearly set out in the Guidelines (see, *e.g.* C-VI, 6), and is essentially a matter for the discretion of the Examining Division.

(c) Withdrawal of a request

4–40   A request for oral proceedings may be withdrawn at any time. However, such a withdrawal should be made clearly and as early as possible, and well in advance of the appointed day.

In *inter partes* proceedings, if one party withdraws a request for oral proceedings at a late stage and causes unnecessary expense to other parties, an award of costs under Article 104 EPC may be made.

---

[56] See T34/90 O.J. EPO 1992, 454.
[57] T299/86 O.J. EPO 1988, 88.

If oral proceedings are appointed as a result of a party's request for such proceedings and if that party subsequently states that it will not be represented at the oral proceedings, such a statement is normally treated as equivalent to a withdrawal of the request for oral proceedings.[58]

(d) Summons to oral proceedings

The procedure by which a date for oral proceedings is fixed is currently **4–41** governed by a Notice dated February 14, 1989.[59] According to this procedure, the initiative for proposing a date is initially with the EPO, and normally a definite date is proposed, together with two alternative dates (within the same week for a Board of Appeal hearing), which may be accepted if there are strong reasons preventing a party from attending on the definite date proposed. Objections to the definite date are required within 10 days, and the proposed alternative date should be agreed with all parties to the proceedings beforehand.

This procedure is applied rather strictly, in view of the increasing number of hearings which have to be appointed.

Consequently, if no objections are received within 10 days, a summons to oral proceedings under Rule 71 EPC is issued naming the date initially proposed by the EPO. At least two months' notice of the summons shall be given unless the parties agree to a shorter period (Rule 71(1) EPC).

It is only in "unexpected and exceptional circumstances" (*e.g.* serious illness) that a change of date from that stated in a summons is acceptable.

(e) Failure to appear

Rule 71(2) EPC provides that: "If a party who has been summoned to **4–42** oral proceedings . . . does not appear as summoned, the proceedings may continue without him". Thus, a party cannot delay the issue of a decision in a case by failing to appear at oral proceedings to which it has been summoned. However, if new facts or evidence are presented during oral proceedings in the absence of a party, a decision which is adverse to the absent party and which is based upon such new facts or evidence cannot be issued without first giving the absent party an opportunity to present its comments upon the new facts or evidence, in accordance with Article 113(1) EPC.[60]

(f) Public nature of oral proceedings

Oral proceedings normally take place in public. Exceptions are set out in **4–43** Article 116(3) and (4) EPC.

In particular, under Article 116(3) EPC, proceedings before the Receiving Section, the Examining Division and the Legal Division are not held in

---

[58] T3/90 O.J. EPO 1992, 737.
[59] O.J. EPO 1989, 132.
[60] G4/92 O.J. EPO 1994, 149.

public. These are all *ex parte* proceedings, and are commonly prior to publication of the European patent application.

Under Article 116(4) EPC, oral proceedings before the Opposition Division, and before the Boards of Appeal and the Enlarged Board of Appeal may not be in public if it is decided that "the admission of the public could have serious and unjustified disadvantages, in particular for a party to the proceedings."

E. THE DECISION

(a) Making the decision

4–44   Articles 13 and 14 RPBA provides that when necessary, namely if the members of a Board are not all of the same opinion, decisions on issues in a case are taken by majority vote.

Deliberations within a Board are secret. The Chairman of a Board "may authorise other officers to attend," but in practice this is limited to the authorisation of an assistant to a particular Board to participate in such deliberations.

The order of voting is regulated by Article 14(2) RPBA, in particular, the rapporteur votes first, and the chairman votes last (even if he is also the rapporteur). Abstentions are not permitted.

(b) Issuing the decision

(i) Timing

4–45   In the event of oral proceedings, "the decision may be given orally," in which case "subsequently, the decision in writing shall be notified to the parties" (Rule 68(1) EPC).

In practice, at the conclusion of oral proceedings normally only the bare decision on the issues is announced, corresponding to the "order" in the written decision, and the reasons for the decision are issued later in writing.

In accordance with Article 11(3) RPBA the policy is that the procedure should lead to a situation in which the case is ready for decision at the conclusion of oral proceedings. Thus, in almost all appeals involving oral proceedings the result is announced orally. However, in appropriate cases a Board may reserve its decision.

Whether or not oral proceedings have taken place, the written decision is drafted by the rapporteur, agreed with the other members of the Board and issued to each party. Every written decision must be in accordance with Rule 66(2) EPC. The composition of the Board of Appeal responsible for decision is set out on the title page, with the Chairman first and the rapporteur second. No dissenting opinions are issued (*cf.* the Enlarged Board of Appeal, as to which see paragraph 4–51 below).

(ii) Maintenance with amended text—special considerations

In an opposition appeal, if the final decision of the Board of Appeal is to maintain the patent in an amended text, the requirements of Rule 58(4) and (5) EPC in respect of a written communication have been interpreted as intended to ensure that due account is taken in opposition proceedings of the principles of due process set out in Article 113 EPC.[61]

Thus, after oral proceedings in connection with an opposition, the parties must be sent a communication pursuant to Rule 58(4) EPC only if they cannot reasonably be expected to state their observations concerning the maintenance of the European patent in the amended from definitively during the oral proceedings.[62]

A written communication under Rule 58(4) EPC after oral proceedings is therefore frequently dispensed with.

(c) Finality of a decision

Once a decision has been issued, whether orally or in writing, it is final **4-46** and cannot be cancelled or changed by the instance which issued it.[63] This is subject to the correction of errors under Rule 89 EPC, which provides that "only linguistic errors, errors of transcription and obvious mistakes may be corrected."

The decision of a Board of Appeal is binding upon the first instance department who issued the decision under appeal, not only as regards the "order" made, but also as regards the *ratio decidendi* of the decision of the Board of Appeal, insofar as the facts are the same (Article 111(2) EPC).

Neither an Examining Division nor a Board of Appeal has power to re-open examination of claims which have previously been refused by the Board of Appeal.[64]

Furthermore, no possibility of an appeal from a decision of a Board of Appeal is provided by the EPC (although points decided in earlier decisions of Boards of Appeal may subsequently be referred to the Enlarged Board of Appeal for opinion or decision—see paragraphs 4-49 *et seq*. below). In particular, there is no provision for any further appeal to a court outside the EPO.

(d) Costs in oppositions, including appeals

The general principle with respect to costs is set out in Article 104(1) **4-47** EPC as follows:

"Each party to the proceedings shall meet the costs he has incurred unless a decision of an Opposition Division or Board of Appeal, for reasons of equity, orders a different apportionment of costs incurred, either

(i) during taking of evidence
(ii) or in oral proceedings."

---

[61] T219/83 O.J. EPO 1986, 211.
[62] T185/84 O.J. EPO 1986, 373.
[63] T212/88 O.J. EPO 1992, 28.
[64] T79/89 O.J. EPO 1992, 283; T843/91 (August 5, 1993) O.J. EPO 1994, 832.

(i) "During taking of evidence"

The phrase "taking of evidence" in Article 104(1) EPC, refers generally to the receiving of evidence during opposition proceedings, whatever the form of such evidence, and includes unsworn statements in writing and other documentary evidence.[65]

(ii) "In oral proceedings"

The phrase "oral proceedings" covers costs incurred in or relating to the attendance of oral proceedings.[66]

(iii) "For reasons of equity"

Awards of costs under each of the above headings can only be made "for reasons of equity."

Costs are awarded if a party to proceedings caused unnecessary expense that could well have been avoided with normal care. For example, the late filing of facts and evidence by an opponent has frequently been the basis of an award.

(iv) Requesting costs

A request for costs should normally be made in writing. If made at an oral hearing, the request should be made as part of a party's submissions, and before the decision is announced.[67]

(v) Fixing the costs

The procedure for this is set out in Rule 63 EPC. Either a proportion of a party's costs, or a fixed amount[68] may be awarded.

(e) Refund of an appeal fee—substantial procedural violation

(i) Introduction

4–48　　The appeal fee may be refunded in the event of interlocutory revision under Article 109 EPC (see paragraph 4–22). Rule 67 EPC also provides for reimbursement of the appeal fee in the following circumstances:
(1) The appeal is allowable and
(2) Reimbursement is equitable by reason of a substantial procedural violation.

(ii) A procedural violation

There must have been a procedural violation, as opposed to an error of judgment, in relation to the case.[69]

---

[65] T117/86 O.J. EPO 1989, 401; T323/89 O.J. EPO 1992, 169.
[66] T10/82 O.J. EPO 1983, 407.
[67] T212/88 O.J. EPO 1992, 28.
[68] T323/89 O.J. EPO 1992, 169; T934/91 O.J. EPO 1994, 184.
[69] *e.g.* T19/87 O.J. EPO 1988, 286.

A failure to follow the Guidelines is not a procedural violation within the meaning of Rule 67 EPC unless it also constitutes a violation of a rule or principle of procedure governed by an Article or Rule of the EPC.[70]

Furthermore, in the absence of established case law concerning a particular procedure under the EPC, use of an incorrect procedure does not constitute a substantial procedural violation.[71]

(iii) A substantial violation

A trivial procedural violation by the EPO cannot justify reimbursement of an appeal fee. For example, an alleged violation affecting a part of a decision other than its *ratio decidendi* cannot be a substantial violation within the meaning of Rule 67 EPC.[72]

(iv) Particular examples of "substantial procedural violation"

Violation of Article 113(1) EPC. Article 113(1) EPC provides that a decision of the EPO "may only be based on grounds or evidence on which the parties concerned have had an opportunity to present their comments".

For example, due process of law required by Article 113 EPC has not been applied when a decision to refuse an application is based essentially on documents which, though supplied by the applicant in support of his case, are used against him to produce an effect on which he has not had an opportunity to make observations.[73]

Similarly, if the EPO has examined facts of its own motion, Article 113(1) EPC requires that the parties concerned are fully informed about the enquiries made and the results thereof and then given sufficient opportunity to present their comments before any decision is issued.[74]

Furthermore, if the EPO sends a communication which (on a reasonable interpretation) misleads a party into believing that it is not necessary to file observations in reply to new evidence and related argument filed by an opposing party, and if such new evidence and argument then forms the basis for a decision adversely affecting the first party, the latter has not had "an opportunity to present its comments" within the meaning of Article 113(1) EPC.[75]

Other specific procedural violations. Rule 68(2) EPC requires that decisions of the EPO which are open to appeal "shall be reasoned". Consequently, rejection of a request [*e.g.* an auxiliary request] without any reason being given in the decision itself or at least in a preceding communication referred to therein is a substantial procedural violation.[76]

---

[70] T42/84 O.J. EPO 1988, 251.
[71] T156/84 O.J. EPO 1988, 372; T234/86 O.J. EPO 1989, 79.
[72] T5/81 O.J. EPO 1982, 249.
[73] T18/81 O.J. EPO 1985, 166.
[74] J3/90 O.J. EPO 1991, 550.
[75] T669/90 O.J. EPO 1992, 739.
[76] T234/86 O.J. EPO 1989, 79.

A failure by the Examining Division to order interlocutory revision under Article 109 EPC following the submission of significant amendments may justify reimbursement of the appeal fee.[77]

F. The Enlarged Board of Appeal

(a) Introduction

4–49   The Enlarged Board of Appeal for a particular case consists of five legally qualified members and two technically qualified members of the Boards of Appeal (Article 22(2) EPC, *i.e.* a total of seven members including the Chairman.

In accordance with Article 112 EPC, the dual purpose of the Enlarged Board of Appeal is to provide for uniform application of the law within the Boards of Appeal, and to decide important points of law which arise under the EPC. It provides the highest hierarchical level of judicial authority within the EPO, but it is not a further instance of appeal. It is part of the second instance constituted by the Boards of Appeal.[78]

Individual Boards of Appeal are not bound to follow previous decisions of other Boards of Appeal on a point of law such as interpretation of the EPC. They normally do, but they may not. If a Board of Appeal considers it necessary to deviate from an interpretation or explanation of the EPC given in an earlier decision of any Board, the grounds for this deviation shall be given, unless such grounds are in accordance with an earlier opinion or decision of the Enlarged Board of Appeal. The President of the EPO shall be informed of the Board's decision (Article 15(1) RPBA). In this and other circumstances, the Enlarged Board of Appeal may be asked to give a decision of higher authority upon such a point of law.

According to Article 22 EPC, the Enlarged Board of Appeal is responsible for:

(a) deciding points of law referred to it by Boards of Appeal;
(b) giving opinions on points of law referred to it by the President of the EPO.

A decision under Article 22(a) EPC and an opinion under Article 22(b) EPC are of equal authority; it is merely the procedure by which the points of law are referred to the Enlarged Board which is different in the two cases.

(b) Procedure for referring questions of law to the Enlarged Board

4–50   There are two ways in which the Enlarged Board of Appeal can be convened:

---

[77] T268/85 [1989] EPOR 229.
[78] T79/89 O.J. EPO 1992, 283.

(i) By a Board of Appeal

Under Article 112(1)(a) EPC, an individual Board of Appeal shall refer any questions of law to the Enlarged Board for decision during the course of particular appeal proceedings before it, either of its own motion or upon the request of a party to the appeal proceedings if it considers that such a decision is required in order to ensure uniform application of the law, or in view of the importance of the question.

The following are examples of circumstances when a Board of Appeal may decide to refer a question of law to the Enlarged Board:

(1) If two or more deviating Board of Appeal decisions already exist on such question;

(2) if one or more Board of Appeal decisions in one direction already exist on a point of law, and a Board of Appeal doubts the correctness of such decision(s);

(3) if no decision on a point of law exists, and a Board of Appeal considers it sufficiently important that the Enlarged Board should decide it first.

Time for making a request for referral. A party must request referral of a point of law to the Enlarged Board during proceedings before a Board of Appeal, and before any decision is made relating to the point of law.

After a Board of Appeal has issued a decision in respect of certain issues, it has no power under Article 112(1)(a) EPC in the same proceedings to refer a question of law to the Enlarged Board of Appeal which arose in connection with issues which it has already decided, even though other issues are still pending before the Board of Appeal in proceedings on the same case.[79]

Form of a request. To improve the chances of a request being acceded to, party should not merely make a bare request: he should also state his reasons in support of his request. These will normally include:

(a) the point of law which is said to arise: this can conveniently be put in the form of the draft question(s) which the party wishes to be referred to the Enlarged Board; and

(b) the reasons why the point of law is important and needs to be referred in order to ensure uniform application of the law.

If the Board of Appeal rejects such a request, Article 112(1) EPC required that it must give its reasons in its final decision.

Decision of referral and subsequent procedure. If a Board of Appeal decides to refer one or more questions to the Enlarged Board, either of its own motion or upon request from a party, it issues a written decision (see Article 17 RPBA) setting out a summary of facts and the background to the questions which are to be referred, and the reasons for the referral. The context of the referred questions is thus stated. The appeal proceedings

---

[79] T79/89 O.J. EPO 1992, 283.

before that Board of Appeal are then stayed during the appeal procedure before the Enlarged Board and until the issue of its decision by which the referred questions are decided (Article 22(1)(a) EPC).

The parties to the appeal proceedings before the referring Board of Appeal are automatically parties in the proceedings before the Enlarged Board (Article 112(2) EPC).

The decision which is issued by the Enlarged Board under this procedure is binding on the Board of Appeal which referred the question in respect of the particular appeal concerned (Article 112(3) EPC).

(vi) By the President of the EPO

Under Article 112(1)(b) EPC, the President of the EPO may refer an important point of law to the Enlarged Board "where two Boards of Appeal have given different decisions on that question", in circumstances such as discussed above, in order to ensure uniform application of the law. Since the previous conflicting decisions are already final, such a reference to the Enlarged Board has no effect upon the cases which were the subject of such previous decisions.

The procedure in these circumstances is governed by the same Rules of Procedure as in a referral by a Board. The Enlarged Board is responsible for issuing an "opinion" on the point of law, rather than a decision, and is thus acting in effect as an advisory body, because no particular case is brought before it and there are no parties involved.

(c) Procedure of the Enlarged Board of Appeal

4–51   This is governed primarily by the "Rules of Procedure of the Enlarged Board of Appeal" (RPEBA).[80]

These Rules of Procedure are adopted by the Enlarged Board itself (Article 23(4) and Rule 11 EPC). They are generally similar to those of the Boards of Appeal.

The Enlarged Board may, on its own initiative or at the written, reasoned request of the President of the European Patent Office, invite him to comment in writing or orally on questions of general interest which arise in the course of proceedings pending before it. This procedure enables the President to obtain the views of the relevant department of the EPO on questions of general interest, and to communicate such views to the Enlarged Board. The Enlarged Board will then hear the parties' comments on such views, before deciding a case. The President does not thereby become a party to the proceedings.

During proceedings before it, the Enlarged Board may consider written statements from third parties concerning points of law which are the subject of such proceedings, as it thinks fit.

A decision or opinion of the Enlarged Board may include an indication of the result which would have been preferred by a minority of its members, together with reasons in support.

---

[80] O.J. EPO 1989, 362.

(d) Binding effect of an Enlarged Board decision or opinion

If a question of law is referred to the Enlarged Board of Appeal by an 4–52
individual Board of Appeal during the course of appeal proceedings before
it, either of its own motion or following a request from a party to the
appeal, the decision of the Enlarged Board which answers the referred
question is binding on the Board of Appeal which referred the question in
respect of the appeal in question (Article 112(3) EPC).

Beyond this, however, every Enlarged Board opinion or decision has a
binding effect upon subsequent individual Boards of Appeal, having regard
in particular to Article 16 RPBA which states the following:

"Should a Board consider it necessary to deviate from an interpretation
or explanation of the EPC contained in an earlier opinion or decision of
the Enlarged Board of Appeal, the question shall be referred to the
Enlarged Board of Appeal."

5. Procedural Remedies

CONTENTS

A. INTRODUCTION

Within the system for granting and opposing European patents provided   **5–01** by the EPC, there are many procedural requirements coupled with time limits imposed upon parties to proceedings before the EPO, with accompanying sanctions if such requirements are not complied with in due time. In order to ensure that procedure before the EPO is efficient and runs smoothly, which is in the public interest, the sanctions are frequently severe: immediate loss of a patent application or patent, for example, or the loss of a right such as the right to appeal.

The EPC includes provisions which may alleviate the initial, necessarily strict, requirements of the system in relation to time limits.

One particular class of provisions ensures an automatic further period of time upon payment of a further fee or surcharge. Examples of such provisions are:

(a) Further processing

Article 121 EPC provides that: **5–02**

"If the European patent application is to be refused or is refused or deemed to be withdrawn following failure to reply within a time limit set by the European Patent Office, the legal consequence provided for shall not ensue or, if it has already ensued, shall be retracted if the applicant requests further processing of the application".

This provision is applicable to time limits which are set by the EPO but is not applicable to time limits laid down in the EPC itself. Furthermore, this provision is not applicable during opposition proceedings, since it is concerned only with a European patent application. In order to obtain further processing of an application, the only requirements are that within two months of expiry of the date on which either the decision to refuse the application or the communication that the application is deemed to be withdrawn is notified, a request in writing for further processing must be filed, a prescribed fee must be paid, and the omitted act must be completed.

(b) Late payment of renewal fees

5–03 These may be made, together with an additional fee, within six months of the due date (Article 86(2) EPC).

(c) Late payment of filing, search, designation, national and request for examination fees

5–04 These may be made, together with a surcharge, within a grace period (Rules 85(a) and (b) EPC).

The requirements in relation to such provisions are not discussed further. This chapter is concerned with three particular crcumstances where special remedies are provided by the EPC in the event of procedural failures, namely: the correction of mistakes in formal documents (Rule 88 EPC, first sentence); the re-establishment of rights (Article 122 EPC); and the interruption of proceedings (Rule 90 EPC).

B. The Correction of Errors and Mistakes in Formal Documents: Rule 88 EPC, First Sentence

(a) Introduction

5–05 Rule 88 EPC provides that "Linguistic errors, errors of transcription and mistakes in any document filed with the EPO may be corrected on request."

Although not explicit in this provision, the correction of such errors and mistakes is normally associated with the fact that the error or mistake has not been noticed before the expiry of a relevant time limit. If an error or mistake in a document is recognised before expiry of a time limit in relation to such document, a corrected document can normally be substituted within the time limit.

For the purpose of Rule 88 EPC, a mistake may be said to exist if a document does not express the true intention of the person on whose behalf it was filed. The application of Rule 88 EPC involves three aspects:

(a) it must be established that either an error of the kind set out or a mistake was made;

(b) the error or mistake must be in a document;

(c) correction of the error or mistake is discretionary.

These different aspects will be discussed separately below.

The second sentence of Rule 88 EPC, concerning the correction of obvious mistakes in a description, claims or drawings, is considered separately in paragraphs 7–26 et seq. below.

(b) Evidence of the existence of an error or mistake

5–06 In order to establish that a correction should be allowed, the burden is on the applicant to establish that a mistake has been made and what the mistake was.[1] Account must be taken of all the facts and evidence which

---

[1] J8/80 O.J. EPO 1980, 293.

enables the applicant's intention to be established; consideration is not limited to the documents already on file. Thus, evidence of all relevant facts should be filed in support of an application for correction.[2]

(c) A mistake which is not in a filed document (*e.g.* a non-payment) is not correctable under Rule 88 EPC

Failure to pay a fee within a required time limit, when payment was intended, is an example of a mistake of fact which cannot be corrected under Rule 88 EPC.[3]   5–07

(d) Particular kinds of mistakes

(i) Naming the wrong applicant or opponent

Such mistakes may in principle be corrected.[4]   5–08

(ii) Mistakes in the designation of States

Introduction. Article 79(1) and Rule 26(2)(h) EPC require that the "request for grant" shall contain "the designation of the Contracting State or States in which protection of the invention is desired." A number of cases under Rule 88 EPC concern incorrect designations, such as particular States having allegedly been omitted by mistake. The correction of such omissions has been of considerable importance in a number of cases, since allowing an additional designation after the date of filing is equivalent to a new national patent application.   5–09

Article 79(3) EPC allows the designation of a Contracting State to be withdrawn at any time up to a grant of a European patent. Designation fees are not refunded.

Effect of publication of the application: time limitation. A correction of a designation can in principle only be allowed if the request for correction is received by the EPO in sufficient time to enable publication of a warning concerning the existence of the application for correction together with the European patent application.[5] This applies even when the applicant has requested correction immediately upon discovering the existence of the mistake.[6]   5–10

Precautionary designation of all States. The current "Request for Grant" form includes a pre-printed precautionary designation of all Contracting States, in order to avoid problems concerning the omission of States by mistake.   5–11

---

[2] J4/85 O.J. EPO 1986, 205.
[3] J21/84 O.J. EPO , 1986, 75; T152/85 O.J. EPO 1987, 191.
[4] J7/80 O.J. EPO 1981, 137; T219/86 O.J. EPO 1988, 254.
[5] J12/80 O.J. EPO 1981, 143; J3/81 O.J. EPO 1982, 100; J21/84 O.J. EPO 1986, 75; J7/90 O.J. EPO 1993, 133.
[6] J7/90 O.J. EPO 1993, 133.

Furthermore, for the purpose of according a filing date under Article 80(b) EPC, there is no need for an explicit designation of any particular Contracting State. In the absence of such a designation, the documents filed by the applicant are considered to contain a precautionary designation of all Contracting States.[7]

5–12 Retraction of a withdrawal of a designation after publication. A correction of a withdrawal of a designation is allowable under Rule 88 EPC in appropriate circumstances, in particular if:

    (a) the public has not been officially notified of the withdrawal by the EPO at the time the retraction of the withdrawal is applied for;

    (b) the erroneous withdrawal is due to an excusable oversight;

    (c) the requested correction does not result in a substantial delay of the proceedings; and

    (d) the EPO is satisfied that the interests of third parties who may possibly have taken notice of the withdrawal by inspection of the file are adequately protected.[8]

5–13 Mistake in the designation as published. In one case an international application under the Patent Cooperation Treaty (PCT) was wrongly interpreted by the International Bureau, so that the published application failed to designate a particular Contracting State, contrary to the proper interpretation of the application as filed. It was held that there had been no mistake in the Request for Grant form, and that no correction of such form was therefore necessary, since the EPO was bound to recognise the designation under Article 153 EPC even though it was not included in the published data.[9]

(iii) Mistakes in claiming priority

5–14 Rule 26(2)(g) EPC requires that the request for grant shall contain "where applicable, a declaration claiming the priority of an earlier application . . .". (as to claiming priority, see Chapter 9). In some cases, such a claim to priority has been incomplete, or omitted altogether. Following publication of a European patent application under Article 93 EPC, the public should be entitled to rely on the published information as being both accurate and complete.[10]

In principle, a request for correction of a priority claim should be made sufficiently early for a warning to third parties to be included in the application as published under Article 93 EPC, if it is to be allowable.[11] Exceptionally, correction has been allowed in particular cases without publication of such a warning; for example, if the EPO fails to publish a

[7] J25/88 O.J. EPO 1989, 486.
[8] J10/87 O.J. EPO 1989, 323.
[9] J26/87 O.J. EPO 1989, 329.
[10] J14/82 O.J. EPO 1983, 121.
[11] J4/82 O.J. EPO 1982, 385; J14/82 O.J. EPO 1983, 121; J3/82 O.J. EPO 1983, 171; J6/91 O.J. EPO 1994, 349.

warning,[12] or it is apparent on the face of the published application that the priority claim is missing or wrong.[13]

C. RESTITUTIO IN INTEGRUM: ARTICLE 122 EPC

(a) Introduction

Article 122 EPC provides a potential remedy for the majority of cases in   5–15 which loss of rights or means of redress is caused by failure to comply with a time limit *vis-à-vis* the EPO.

The EPC provides for a number of procedural steps to be taken within time limits laid down either in the Convention itself or by the EPO. Failure to observe these limits frequently involves the person concerned in an irrevocable loss of rights. This is particularly harsh when that person was not actually at fault and the failure was attributable to an oversight which occurred in spite of all due care required by the circumstances having been taken. *Restitutio in integrum* was instituted to mitigate this hardship.[14]

In contrast to Rule 88 EPC, which is limited in its effect to mistakes concerning documents (see paragraphs 5–05 and 5–07 above), Article 122 EPC is potentially applicable to mistakes of fact, such as the failure to pay a fee in due time. Furthermore, in contrast to Article 121 EPC, which provides for further processing of a European patent application only in a case of non-compliance with a time limit set by the EPO (see paragraph 5–02, above), Article 122 EPC also allows the re-establishment of rights which would otherwise be lost because of non-compliance with a time limit laid down in the EPC itself. Additionally, in contrast to Article 121 EPC, which only concerns the further processing of an application, Article 122 EPC is sometimes applicable in opposition proceedings (see paragraph 5–16 below).

There are, however, certain specified time limits in respect of which re-establishment of rights under Article 122 EPC is not available (see paragraph 5–17 below).

Article 122 EPC sets out both formal and substantive requirements which must be satisfied if re-establishment or rights is to be granted. These are discussed separately below. The substantive requirement is that "in spite of all due care required by the circumstances having been taken, [a person] was unable to observe a time limit . . .".

(b) Whose rights may be re-established?

Article 122(1) EPC specifies that "The applicant for or proprietor of" a   5–16 European patent may apply to have his rights re-established.

An opponent may also apply for re-establishment of rights following failure to comply with the time limit for filing a statement of grounds of

---

[12] J14/82 O.J. EPO 1983, 121.
[13] J3/91, J6/91, J2/92 O.J. EPO 1994, 349, 365, 375.
[14] G1/86 O.J. EPO 1987, 447.

appeal under Article 108 EPC, in appeal proceedings where the notice of appeal has been filed in due time.[15] An opponent may not apply for re-establishment of rights following failure to comply with the time limit for filing a notice of appeal under Article 108 EPC,[16] or following failure to comply with the time limit of filing a notice of opposition under Article 99 EPC.[17]

It is possible that other parties to proceedings before the EPO may also have their rights re-established (*e.g.* representatives under Article 20 EPC, inventors under Rule 19 EPC, and lawful applicants under Article 61 EPC).[18]

(c) Circumstances when re-establishment is not available

(i) Excluded time limits

5–17   Article 122(5) EPC identifies certain time limits set by the EPC to which re-establishment of rights is not applicable. These excluded time limits are in respect of:

(a) filing an application for re-establishment under Article 122(2) EPC itself;

(b) paying filing, search and examination fees in respect of a new European patent application filed under Article 61(1)(b) EPC when it is found that a person other than the applicant is entitled to grant of a patent;

(c) paying the filing, search and examination fees in respect of a divisional application under Article 76 EPC;

(d) paying the filing and search fees in respect of a European patent application under Article 78(3) EPC (including the period of grace under Rule 85(a) EPC)[19];

(e) paying the designation fee in respect of a European patent application under Article 79(2) EPC (including the period of grace under Rule 85(a) EPC)[20];

(f) filing a European patent application within the twelve-month priority period in order to claim a right of priority from an earlier application under Article 87(1) EPC;

(g) filing a request for examination (including paying the fee) in respect of a European patent application under Article 94(2) EPC (including the period of grace under Rule 85(b) EPC).[21]

The time limits identified in paragraphs (d), (e) and (g) are also excluded under Article 122 EPC when an initial international application is made under the Patent Cooperation Treaty (PCT), and then becomes the subject

[15] *Ibid.*
[16] T210/89 O.J. EPO 1991, 433.
[17] T25/85 O.J. EPO 1986, 81; T152/85 O.J. EPO 1987, 191; T702/89 O.J. EPO 1994, 472.
[18] G1/86 O.J. EPO 1987, 447.
[19] J18/82 O.J. EPO 1983, 441.
[20] *Ibid.*
[21] J12/82 O.J. EPO 1983, 221.

of examination proceedings before the EPO by virtue of Article 150(2) EPC.[22]

(ii) When rights are lost by virtue of a time limit not imposed upon an applicant

Article 122 EPC provides only for re-establishment of rights where there **5–18** has been a failure to observe a time limit which it has been for the applicant to observe.[23]

(iii) When no rights are lost as a direct consequence of non-observance of a time limit

If a failure to observe a time limit under the EPC can be corrected as a **5–19** deficiency under Article 91 EPC within a further period of time specified under Rule 41 EPC, and is so corrected, there is no loss of rights and Article 122 EPC is not applicable.[24]

(d) Time limits in connection with *restitutio in integrum*

(i) For filing an application for re-establishment

There are two aspects to the time limit for filing an application under **5–20** Article 122(2) EPC:

(1) The application for re-establishment must be filed within two months from "the removal of the cause of non-compliance [with the original time limit]". The meaning of the phrase "removal of the cause of non-compliance" is considered in paragraphs 5–22 below.

(2) The application for re-establishment must also be filed within the year immediately following the expiry of the unobserved time limit. This is an absolute time limit, in the interest of legal certainty,[25] subject to one specific exception provided in Article 122(2) EPC, namely in a case where a renewal fee is not paid before the due date under Article 86 EPC. In such a case, the period of six months specified in Article 86(2) EPC, during which the renewal fee plus an additional fee may be paid, is deducted from the one year period of Article 122(2) EPC, with the result that an application for re-establishment must be filed within six months of the due date for payment of the renewal fee plus additional fee.

To make a valid application within this one year period, it is sufficient if the file contains a clearly documented statement of intent from which the public may infer that the applicant is trying to maintain the application.[26]

---

[22] G3/91 O.J. EPO 1993, 8 overruling J6/79 O.J. EPO 1980, 225 and J5/80 O.J. EPO 1981, 343.
[23] J3/80 O.J. EPO 1980, 92.
[24] J1/80 O.J. EPO 1980, 289.
[25] J16/86 December 1, 1986.
[26] J6/90 O.J. EPO 1993, 714.

(ii) For completion of the omitted act

5–21   The second sentence of Article 122(2) EPC states that "The omitted act must be completed within this period", that is, within the two month period which begins with the "removal of the cause of non-compliance" with the time limit.

Thus, determination of the date of removal of the cause of non-compliance is frequently important in connection with the admissibility of applications for re-establishment, having regard to the non-extensibility of the time limits for filing such an application (subject to interruption under Rule 90 EPC – see paragraphs 5–22 and 5–32 to 5–37 below).

(iii) Interruption of the time limits under Article 122 EPC

5–22   The only possibility of filing an admissible application for re-establishment after expiry of the above two-month and one-year time limits is in the case of an interruption of proceedings under Rule 90 EPC[27] (see paragraph 5–32 et seq. below).

(iv) Purpose of the two-month period

5–23   The two-month period laid down in Article 122 EPC was designed to enable parties to carry out the necessary investigations and consultations, as well as to prepare the documentation for submission of a request under Article 122 EPC. The date of removal of the cause of non-compliance cannot, therefore, be set at the date when these preparations have been completed and the representative is about to submit a request for re-establishment, but must be a date before that.[28]

(v) Removal of the cause of non-compliance

5–24   The starting point for the relatively short period of two months is defined by reference to the "removal of the cause of non-compliance." The determination of this starting date depends upon the particular circumstances involved, and it is impossible to decide what is the cause of non-compliance with a time limit without considering the facts of each case.[29] Some particular circumstances are considered below.

Notification of non-observance.   Frequently, a party or his representative has intended to comply with a time limit and is unaware that the time limit was not in fact observed until receipt of some kind of notification from the EPO to the effect that loss of rights has occurred as a result of non-observance. In such a case, it is the fact (i.e. the date) of actual receipt by the applicant which is significant, not the fact of despatch by the EPO.[30]

---

[27] J.../87 O.J. EPO 1988, 323.
[28] J17/89 January 9, 1990.
[29] Ibid.
[30] J7/82 O.J. EPO 1982, 391.

Knowledge of non-observance before receipt of notification. The date of removal of the cause of non-compliance is the date of knowledge of non-observance, if this date is before receipt of a notification from the EPO.[31]

Knowledge of non-observance by the person responsible. In the absence of circumstances to the contrary a communication to the European professional representative appointed under Article 133(2) EPC (see paragraphs 2–05 and 3–09) removes the cause of non-compliance. This applies when a European professional representative is instructed by a national patent attorney. Furthermore, the professional representative remains responsible even if an independent service firm is made responsible for the payment of fees.[32]

In a case in which non-compliance with a time limit leading to a loss of rights under the EPC is discovered by an employee of a representative, the cause of non-compliance, *i.e.* failure to appreciate that the time limit has not been complied with, cannot be considered to have been removed until the representative concerned has himself been made aware of the facts, since it must be his responsibility to decide whether an application for re-establishment of rights should be made and, if it is to be made, to determine the grounds and supporting facts to be presented to the EPO.[33]

(e) Contents of the application for re-establishment

According to Article 122(2) and (3) EPC, the application for re- 5–25 establishment must be in writing, must state "the grounds on which it is based", and must set out "the facts on which it relies". If these requirements are not complied with within the specified time limits, the application may be considered inadmissible.

In order to comply with the two-month time limit laid down in Article 122(2) EPC, it is not necessary that the application for re-establishment of rights provides any prima facie evidence for the facts set out in it, not is it necessary that it indicates the means by which those facts are supported (*e.g.* medical certificates, sworn statements and the like). Such evidence may be submitted after the time limit, if so required.[34]

(f) Contents of grounds of appeal equivalent to an application for re-establishment

In exceptional circumstances, where the applicant had become confused 5–26 as to the correct procedure to be followed after the issue of a decision of revocation under Article 102(4) and (5) EPC, a statement of grounds of appeal effectively setting out grounds for re-establishment has been accepted as an application for re-establishment.[35]

---

[31] J17/89, January 9, 1990.
[32] J27/90 O.J. EPO 1993, 422.
[33] T191/82 O.J. EPO 1985, 189.
[34] T324/90 O.J. EPO 1993, 33.
[35] T14/89 O.J. EPO 1990, 432.

In principle, however, grounds of appeal are the antithesis of grounds for re-establishment, since the former should be setting out a case for why the appellant should not have lost rights or otherwise been "adversely affected", and the latter should be setting out a case why in the particular circumstances rights which have been lost should be re-established.[36]

(g) "All due care required by the circumstances"

(i) Introduction

5–27   Article 122(1) EPC provides that if the party concerned "was unable to observe a time limit . . . in spite of all due care required by the circumstances having been taken", then rights which are lost as a direct consequence of the non-observance shall be re-established.

Thus, the onus is upon an applicant for re-establishment of rights to prove that the non-observance of the time limit happened in spite of "all due care" having been taken to observe it.

Determination of this question necessarily involves consideration of the particular facts of each case, and since the facts of a case are rarely exactly the same as a previous one, a detailed classification of the many Board of Appeal decisions concerning this matter would be inappropriate. Nevertheless, some particular factual circumstances are discussed below.

(ii) Mistakes in a system

5–28   The majority of applications for re-establishment are consequential upon a mistake or error having been made either by the applicant or proprietor himself or by his representative. In many cases, the applicant, proprietor or representative is responsible for the prosecution of many patent applications or patents, and for observing many time limits in connection therewith, and something unusual happens so as to cause a particular time limit to be missed.

Article 122 EPC is intended to ensure that in appropriate cases the loss of substantive rights does not result from an isolated procedural mistake within a normally satisfactory system.[37]

Thus, in cases of this type, a Board of Appeal will normally examine whether the system of reminders, cross-checks, etc., which is used to ensure compliance with the relegvant time limits, can properly be considered as a normally satisfactory system.

Applicants, proprietors and professional representatives commonly employ assistants to perform tasks which are part of the system for ensuring compliance with time limits. It is encumbent upon the representative to choose for the work a suitable person, properly instructed in the tasks to be performed, and to exercise reasonable supervision over the work. If this has been done the same strict standards of care are not

---

[36] T522/88 December 19, 1989.
[37] J2, 3/86 O.J. EPO 1987, 362.

expected of the assistant as are expected of the applicant or his representative. Nevertheless, if the representative delegates to an assistant a task which normally falls to him, as, for example the interpretation of laws and treaties, all due care would not have been established.[38]

(iii) Inadequate professional advice

For an applicant who himself is lacking the necessary knowledge of procedures, failure to consult a competent professional representative may constitute a lack of due care.[39]   5–29

(iv) Financial difficulties

Unavoidable financial difficulties which result in failure to observe time limits for payment of fees may constitute grounds for granting re-establishment of rights, provided the requester has exercised all due care in seeking financial assistance.[40]   5–30

(h) The department competent to decide

According to Article 122(4) EPC, "The department competent to decide on the omitted act shall decide upon the application" (for re-establishment). Thus, in the majority of cases, a first instance department of the EPO is responsible for deciding upon an application for re-establishment, and its decision may be the subject of an appeal in the usual way.   5–31

When a time limit is not observed in the course of appeal proceedings, for example the four-month time limit for filing a statement of grounds of appeal, the Board of Appeal is itself competent to decide upon such an omitted act and consequently upon an application for re-establishment in connection therewith. There is no possibility of any subsequent appeal.

D. INTERRUPTION OF PROCEEDINGS: RULE 90 EPC

(a) Introduction

If certain events which are defined in Rule 90(1) EPC occur, "proceedings before the EPO shall be interrupted." In effect, time stops running as a result of such an interruption. New time limits which apply after the proceedings are resumed are then determined.   5–32

(b) Events which result in interruption

These are specified in Rule 90(1) EPC as follows: 5–33

---

[38] J5/80 O.J. EPO 1981, 343.
[39] J23/87 [1987] EPOR, 52.
[40] J22/88 O.J. EPO 1990, 244.

(a) death or legal incapacity of the applicant or proprietor, or the person authorised by national law to act on his behalf;

(b) the applicant or proprietor being prevented by legal reasons from continuing the proceedings, as a result of some action being taken against his property;

(c) death or legal incapacity of the representative of the applicant or proprietor, or the representative being prevented by legal reasons from continuing the proceedings, resulting from action taken against his property.

Thus, it seems that opponents or other parties to proceedings before the EPO are not entitled to claim interruption of proceedings in which they are taking part.

(c) Automatic nature of an interruption

5–34   Rule 90 EPC must be applied automatically by the EPO, of its own motion; no specific formalities are required.[41]

(d) The meaning of "legal incapacity"

5–35   The means of determining the legal incapacity of an applicant or proprietor (Rule 90(1)(a) EPC) on the one hand, and a representative (Rule 90(1)(c) EPC) on the other hand, have to be distinguished.

The legal capacity of the applicant or proprietor to carry out legal transactions relating to his application or patent must be determined according to a national system of law, since his interest in the application or patent is an interest in property.

The question of the capacity of a representative is clearly different. The relevant aspect of his legal incapacity for the purposes of Rule 90(1)(c) EPC is that of his incapacity to carry out professional work on behalf of a client. The question is whether the representative concerned was in a fit mental state to do the work required of him at the material time or whether he lacked the capacity to make rational decisions and to take necessary actions.[42]

For a representative, incapacity to carry out professional work before the EPO must be of a persistent nature.[43]

(e) The meaning of a "representative"

5–36   The legal incapacity of a patent attorney from outside the Contracting States may be that of a representative for the purpose of causing an interruption of proceedings pursuant to Rule 90(1)(c) EPC.[44]

---

[41] J.../87 O.J. EPO 1988, 323.
[42] J/Unnumbered O.J. EPO 1985, 159.
[43] J.../86 O.J. EPO 1987, 528.
[44] J23/88 April 25, 1989.

(f) The effect of an interruption upon a time limit

(i) Introduction

Calculation of the time limits which have to be observed in the event of 5–37 an interruption of proceedings depends upon the interpretation of Rule 90(1) and (4) EPC. Rule 90(4) EPC includes two exceptions in this respect, namely in connection with the time limits for making a request for examination and for paying renewal fees: these exceptions are considered separately below.

(ii) General rule for determination of the new time limit

In general, on the day when the proceedings are resumed, the period of the time limit also begins to run again.[45]

(iii) Two exceptions: request for examination and renewal fees

Request for examination. In this case, the interrupted time limit must necessarily resume for the remaining time only.[46] However, under Rule 90(4) EPC, as regards the filing of a request for examination, "the time remaining at the applicant's disposal may in no circumstances be shorter than two months."

Renewal fees. In this case, however, Rule 90(4) EPC has to be interpreted as deferring the payment date for renewal fees falling due during the period of incapacity of the applicant or his representative until the date proceedings are resumed.[47]

---

[45] J7/83 O.J. EPO 1984, 211.
[46] Ibid.
[47] J.../87 O.J. EPO 1988, 323.

6. The Contents of a European Patent Application

A. INTRODUCTION

(a) Prescribed contents

According to Article 78 EPC, a European patent application must **6–01** contain (in addition to a request for grant of a European patent):

(i) a description;
(ii) one or more claims;
(iii) any drawings referred to in the description or the claims;
(iv) an abstract.

(b) Drawings

Any drawings are clearly ancillary to the description and/or the claims **6–02** (normally the description). Drawings are, however, part of the substantive contents of an application.

(c) Abstract

An abstract must be provided by an applicant in order to comply with **6–03** Article 78 EPC (although it is not necessary for allocation of a filing date – Article 80 EPC). Article 85 EPC makes the limited purpose of an abstract clear, namely that it "shall merely serve for use as technical information: it may not be taken into account for any other purpose, in particular, not for the purpose of interpreting the scope of the protection sought not for the purpose of applying Article 54(3) EPC."

The abstract is not part of the substantive contents of an application and cannot be taken into account when determining what subject matter is contained in the application as filed.[1]

The requirements for the substantive contents of an application (*i.e.* the description and the claims, together with any drawings) will be considered below in two parts, first, the description and the corresponding requirement of sufficiency, and secondly, the claims and the corresponding requirements of clarity and support.

B. THE DESCRIPTION AND SUFFICIENCY

(a) The description

(I) Prescribed contents

The contents of a description of a European patent are prescribed in **6–04** detail in Rule 27(1) EPC, the sub-paragraphs of which may be summarised as follows:

---

[1] T407/86 [1988] EPOR 254.

(a) technical field of the invention;
(b) background art;
(c) disclosure of invention as claimed in terms of the technical problem and its solution, stating advantageous effects with reference to background art;
(d) description of drawings;
(e) description of at least one way of carrying out the invention;
(f) how the invention is capable of industrial exploitation.

The above manner and order of the contents of the description should be followed unless the nature of the invention is such that a different manner or order "would afford a better understanding and a more economical presentation" (Rule 27(2) EPC). Individual requirements of this Rule have been held to be mandatory.[2]

(ii) Background art (Rule 27(1)(b) and (c) EPC)

6–05   An applicant must point out or make known the background art known to him, preferebly by mentioning it and/or quoting documents which reflect it.[3]

If a document is part of the common general knowledge and is the closest prior art, it may have to be introduced into the description.[4]

(iii) Examples: at least one way of carrying out the invention (Rule 27(1)(e) EPC)

6–06   Normally, one or more specific examples of how to carry out a claimed invention are included in the description of an application, but this is not mandatory.

(iv) Functions of the description

6–07   These are as follows:

(a) To disclose an invention which satisfies Article 52 EPC;
(b) to provide a sufficient disclosure of how to carry out the invention (Article 83 EPC);
(c) to support the claims (Article 84 EPC).

(b) Sufficiency of disclosure: Article 83 EPC

(i) The basic principle

6–08   According to Article 83 EPC, a European patent application "must disclose the invention in a manner sufficiently clear and complete for it to be carried out by a person skilled in the art". The reference to a person

---

[2] T11/82 O.J. EPO 1983, 479 and T26/81 O.J. EPO 1982, 211.
[3] T11/86 O.J. EPO 1983, 479.
[4] T51/87 O.J. EPO 1991, 177.

skilled in the art ensures that it is unnecessary to include minor details of how to perform an invention, in that such a person inevitably has a body of knowledge in his art (the "common general knowledge") which can be applied as and when appropriate to the disclosure of an invention in a particular patent application.

Such sufficient disclosure must be found in the description and claims in combination (and drawings if any) (*i.e.* in the substantive contents – see paragraphs 6–02 and 6–03 above).

The basic principle in determining questions concerning sufficiency of disclosure is that the claimed invention must be capable of performance by a skilled person, either on the basis of the information in the application on its own, or supplemented when appropriate by information which is part of the commmon general knowledge of such skilled person.

The following examples illustrate particular applications of this principle:

(1) In one case, a process step had been claimed functionally (*i.e.* do something so as to achieve a particular result). The applicant admitted during examination of the application that details of the actual production process had been kept secret to prevent them from being copied from the patent. The disclosure in the application was held to be insufficient under Article 83 EPC because the conditions for achieving the required result were not disclosed, and such missing information was not part of the common general knowledge.[5]

(2) On the other hand, an error in the description (an incorrect numerical value in the only example) does not cause insufficiency of the disclosure if the skilled person could recognise it and rectify it using his common general knowledge.[6]

(ii) The "invention" which must be sufficiently disclosed: preparation of starting materials

It may be necessary for the description to contain a sufficient disclosure 6–09 as to how to obtain the starting materials necessary for the performance of the claimed invention.[7]

(iii) What consititutes common general knowledge?

Patent specifications are normally considered to be outside common 6–10 general knowledge, whereas text books and handbooks are normally considered to be part of the common general knowledge.[8]

The contents of *Chemical Abstracts* (a well-known source of information in the chemical industry) have been held not to be part of the common general knowledge of a chemist.[9]

---

[5] T219/85 O.J. EPO 1986, 376.
[6] T171/84 O.J. EPO 1986, 95.
[7] T206/83 O.J. EPO 1987, 5 (but see T51/87 O.J. EPO 1991, 177 for a contrary view).
[8] T171/84 O.J. EPO 1986, 95 and T206/83 O.J. EPO 1987, 5.
[9] T206/83 O.J. EPO 1987, 5.

In cases concerning newly developing fields of technology, patent specifications[10] and specialist periodicals[11] have been considered as part of the common general knowledge.

(iv) What constitutes undue burden?

6–11   The basic requirement is that a skilled person should be able to carry out an invention from the disclosure of an application without "undue burden."

Occasional lack of success in the performance of a claimed process does not necessarily mean that the description is insufficient, provided that the description contains information which enables corrective action to be taken so as to achieve success quickly and reliably thereafter.[12]

Even though a reasonable amount of trial and error is permissible when it comes to the sufficiency of disclosure in an unexplored field or where there are many technical difficulties, there must then be available adequate instructions in the specification or on the basis of common general knowledge which would lead the skilled person necessarily and directly towards success through the evaluation of initial failures or through an acceptable statistical expectation rate in case of random experiments. If the reason for failure is not known, this may cause an undue burden of experimentation and make the description insufficient.[13]

Information which can only be obtained after a comprehensive search is not to be regarded as part of common general knowledge.[14] In this circumstance, the concept of an "undue burden" can be considered as part of the determination of what constitutes common general knowledge.

(v) How many ways of carrying out the invention must be disclosed?

6–12   It has been held in some cases that an invention is sufficiently disclosed if at least one way is clearly indicated enabling the skilled person to carry out the invention.[15]

However, the need for a fair protection governs both the considerations of the scope of the claims and of the requirements for sufficient disclosure. In other words, the extent of disclosure of ways of performing the claimed invention is related to the scope of the claims, which is in turn related to considerations of providing a fair protection having regard to the nature of the invention in question. While in particular cases the fact that one way of performing the claimed invention has been disclosed in a patent may meet an objection of insufficiency, nevertheless, the requirement of sufficiency is related to the scope of the claims in question in any particular case. The application as filed must contain sufficient information to allow

---

[10] T51/87 O.J. EPO 1991, 177.
[11] T292/85 O.J. EPO 1989, 275.
[12] T14/83 O.J. EPO 1984, 105.
[13] T226/85 O.J. EPO 1988, 336.
[14] T206/83 O.J. EPO 1987, 5.
[15] T292/85 O.J. EPO 1989, 275; T182/89 O.J. EPO 1991, 391; T212/88 O.J. EPO 1992, 28.

a skilled person using his common general knowledge to carry out the invention within the *whole area* that is claimed. The disclosure of an invention is only sufficient if the skilled person can reasonably expect that substantially all embodiments of a claimed invention can be put into practice.[16]

In proceedings before the Examining Division the mere fact that a claim is broad is not in itself a ground for considering the application as insufficient under Article 83 EPC. If there are serious doubts as to the performance of all embodiments of the claimed invention, substantiated by verifiable facts, however, an application may lack sufficient disclosure.[17]

(vi) Future variants of functional features

There is no requirement that all embodiments within the claims should **6–13** be reproducible at will. Thus, an application with claims including functionally defined features is not insufficient on the basis that such features include structures which may be developed in the future and which may themselves involve inventions (and which are therefore not reproducible by the ordinary skilled person).[18]

(vii) Exact repeatability not required

There is no requirement under Article 83 EPC to the effect that a **6–14** specifically described example of a process must be exactly repeatable. Variations in the constitution of an agent used in a process are immaterial to the sufficiency of a disclosure provided the claimed process reliably leads to the desired produce.[19]

As long as the description of the process enables the invention to be put into practice, there is no lack of sufficiency.

Thus, generally applicable chemical or biological processes are not insufficiently described for the sole reason that some starting materials or genetic precursors, *e.g.* a particular DNA or a plasmid, are not readily available to obtain each and every variant of the expected result of the invention, *e.g.* the product, provided the process as such is reproducible.[20]

(c) The deposit of micro-organisms

Introduction

During the period immediately preceding the signing of the EPC, it **6–15** became apparent that with certain inventions involving new strains of micro-organisms it was in practice impossible to describe the micro-organism in writing (and/or with drawings) in such a way that it could be

---

[16] T292/85 O.J. EPO 1989, 275; T409/91 O.J. EPO 1994, 653; T435/91 O.J. EPO (P).
[17] T19/90 O.J. EPO 1990, 476.
[18] T292/85 O.J. EPO 1989, 275.
[19] T281/86 O.J. EPO 1989, 202.
[20] T292/85 O.J. EPO 1989, 275.

obtained or reproduced by a skilled person, and the claimed invention thereby carried out.

In response to this situation, the EPC was drafted to include provisions in the Rules, supplementing the requirement of Article 83 EPC, governing the deposit of micro-organisms in certain recognised institutions so as to supplement the written description of a European patent application. The combination of the written description and the deposited micro-organism was to provide the information necessary for the carrying out of the invention in appropriate cases.

The EPC was the first patent law to include specific provisions in respect of the deposit of micro-organisms as a supplement to the written description of an invention.

A "Notice of the EPO concerning micro-organism patents",[21] dated July 18, 1986, was published in the Official Journal of the EPO in order to assist applicants with the drafting of applications concerning micro-organisms, as well as to explain the procedure concerning requests for samples of deposits and the issues of samples.

(ii) Nature of an invention for which deposit is required

6–16   Rule 28 EPC applies to an invention which:

(a) concerns "a microbiological process or the product thereof";
(b) "and involves the use of a micro-organism which is not available to the public and which cannot be described . . . in such a manner as to enable the invention to be carried out by a person skilled in the art."

(iii) The requirements of Rule 28 EPC

6–17   The requirements of Rule 28 EPC in respect of such an invention may be summarized as follows:

(a) The applicant must deposit a culture of the micro-organism with a recognised depositary institution not later than the filing date.
(b) The application as filed must give "such relevant information as is available to the applicant on the characteristics of the micro-organism."
(c) The depositary institution and the file number of the culture deposit must be stated in the application (this information can be submitted after the filing date–see Rule 28(2) EPC, discussed in paragraph 6–18 below).
(d) The deposited culture must be available upon request from the depositary institution, from the date of publication of the European application.

Requirements (a), (b) and (c) are set out in Rule 28(1) EPC, and requirement (d) – availability – is set out in Rule 28(3) EPC. The

---

[21] Notice of the EPO dated July 18, 1986 concerning European patent applications and European patents in which reference is made to micro-organisms.

requirement of availability of the culture is important, especially as regards when and to whom the deposited micro-organism is made available. The development of the legal requirements in these respects is discussed separately below.

The information required by Rule 28(1)(c) EPC – the depositary institution and the deposit file number – is especially important because as stated in Rule 28(2) EPC, "The communication of this information shall be considered as constituting the unreserved and irrevocable consent of the applicant to the deposited culture being made available to the public . . .".

(iv) Time limit for stating the depositary institution and the file number of deposit

The information required by Rule 28(1)(c) EPC concerning the deposi- **6–18** tary institution and the file number of the culture deposit (which is to be stated in the patent application) may, according to Rule 28(2) EPC, be submitted after the filing of the application, provided it is submitted within the time limits there set out. In particular, in the absence of a request for early publication (Rule 28(2)(b) EPC) and of a communication that a right to inspect the files exists (Rule 28(2)(c) EPC), such information may be submitted within a time limit of 16 months from the filing date (or the priority date if priority is claimed) (Rule 28(2)(a) EPC).

Since Rule 28 EPC supplements the requirements of Article 83 EPC, failure to comply with its time limits will result in refusal of the application for insufficiency under Article 83 EPC.[22]

(v) Deposit in an institution: The Budapest Treaty, 1977[23]

The deposit of a micro-organism for the purpose of a patent application **6–19** must be in an appropriate place and under appropriate control. While deposit for the purpose of a national patent application could appropriately be in a culture collection of the country concerned, that would be unsatisfactory in an international context. Recognition of this led to the signing of the Budapest Treaty concerning the Deposit of Micro-organisms ("Budapest") in 1977. The Treaty has been in force since 1980. It provides (in Article 3 Budapest) for the recognition by Contracting States of the deposit of a micro-organism in any "international depositary authority", by which is meant any depositary institution in a Contracting State which has acquired such status (Article 7 Budapest). The qualifications for such status are set out in Article 6 Budapest, and have now been attained by a considerable number of institutions. The following countries currently have international depositary authorities: Belgium, Bulgaria, Czech

---

[22] G2/93/(P). For earlier conflicting views see J8, 9/87 O.J. EPO 1989, 9, and an Examining Division Decision ("Deposit number") O.J. EPO 1990, 156.

[23] Treaty on the International Recognition of the Deposit of Micro-organisms: "Budapest Treaty."

Republic, France, Germany, Holland, Hungary, Japan, Korea, Russia, Spain, United Kingdom, United States.

So far as European patent applications are concerned, the deposit must be at a "recognised depositary institution" – see requirement (a) above and Rule 28(1)(a) EPC. A list of such recognised institutions is published in the Official Journal – see Rule 28(9) EPC. These include all the institutions which are "international depositary institutions" under the Budapest Treaty and other institutions with which the European Patent Organisation has concluded agreements for this purpose.

Micro-organisms should be deposited in a recognised institution by the applicant. In one case,[24] micro-organisms had been deposited with an institution by a wholly-owned subsidiary of the applicant. It was held that the applicant, the parent company, had control of the deposits, and that these special circumstances justified considering the parent company and subsidiary as one entity for the purpose of Rule 28 EPC.

(vi) Availability of the deposited micro-organism

6–20 **Introduction.** In a general sense, while the deposit of a micro-organism can be considered as corresponding to and supplementing the description of the claimed invention, the making available of what has been deposited to the public can be considered as corresponding to and supplementing the publication of the description. Thus, Rule 28(1)(a) EPC requires deposit not later than the date of filing of an application, and Rule 28(3) requires the deposited micro-organism to be available from the date of publication of the application.

6–21 **Persons to whom available: the "expert option".** Under the original text of Rule 28 EPC when the EPC came into force, a deposited micro-organism had to be made available upon request to "any person", without restriction, from the date of publication of the European patent application. Thus, availability of what was deposited was treated as corresponding exactly to publication of what had been described. Availability was effected by issue of a sample.

However, an amended version of Rule 28 EPC came into force on June 1, 1980, and is still in force, which allows a restriction to be placed upon the class of persons to whom a deposited micro-organism must be made available. In accordance with Rule 28(4) EPC, the applicant for a European patent may inform the EPO before "the technical preparations for publication of the application are deemed to have been completed" that availability "shall be effected only by the issue of a sample to an expert nominated by the requester." This restriction may last until the date of grant (the date of publication of the mention of the grant of the European patent–Article 97(4) EPC) or until refusal, withdrawal or deemed withdrawal of the application. Furthermore, Rule 28(5) EPC places restrictions upon who may be nominated as such an expert, namely either

---

[24] T118/87 O.J. EPO 1991, 474.

(a) an expert approved by the applicant, or

(b) an expert recognised for the purpose by the EPO.

The procedure under Rule 28(4) EPC is known as the "expert option", and is described fully in a "Notice of the President of the EPO" dated July 28, 1981.[25]

Restrictions upon use. Whether or not the "expert option" has been **6–22** exercised, a deposited micro-organism is only made available by issue of a sample thereof (under Rule 28(3) or (4) EPC) subject to an undertaking as set out in Rule 28(3)(a) and (b) EPC, *i.e.*

"(a) not to make the deposited culture or any culture derived therefrom available to any third party before the application has been refused or withdrawn or is deemed to be withdrawn or, if a patent is granted, before the expiry of the patent in the designated State in which it last expires;

(b) to use the deposited culture or any culture derived therefrom for experimental purposes only, until such time as the patent application is refused or withdrawn or is deemed to be withdrawn, or up to the date of publication of the mention of the grant of the European patent."

An undertaking as in (b) is not required if the requester has a compulsory licence (as defined) to use the culture.

(vii) Consequence of non-availability

The exent to which non-compliance with the requirements of Rule 28(3) **6–23** EPC necessarily leads to a finding of insufficiency under Article 83 EPC has been contested in a number of cases before the Boards of Appeal, but no decision has dealt specifically with such contentions.

There may be a deficiency in complying with Rule 28 EPC when the deposit of a culture of a micro-organism, originally made under other legislation, is not converted into a deposit under Rule 28 EPC of the Budapest Treaty, in the manner explained in the Notice[26] concerning micro-organism patents, before the filing of a European patent application.[27]

C. THE CLAIMS: CLARITY AND SUPPORT

(a) Their contents and function

(i) Central role: extent of protection

The EPC contains a single set of provisions which regulates both the **6–24** contents of the claims of a European patent and the relative roles played by the claims, and the description when the extent of protection conferred

---

[25] Notice concerning the "expert option" dated July 28, 1981; O.J. EPO 1981, 358.
[26] See n. 21 above.
[27] T39/88 O.J. EPO 1989, 499.

by the patent is to be determined: this set of provisions is applicable to all patents granted under the EPC, throughout their later life as national patents. These provisions may be summarised as follows. Article 84 EPC provides that the claims of a European patent application "shall define the matter for which protection is sought". Rule 29(1) EPC further requires that the claims "shall define the matter for which protection is sought in terms of the technical features of the invention." The primary aim of the wording used in a claim must therefore be to satisfy such requirements, having regard to the particular nature of the invention, and having regard also to the purpose of such claims.

The purpose of claims under the EPC is to enable the protection conferred by the patent (or patent application) to be determined (Article 69 EPC), and thus the rights of the patent owner within the designated Contracting States (Article 64 EPC), having regard to the patentability requirements of Articles 52 to 57 EPC.[28]

The role of the claims of a European patent is thus central in defining the protection conferred.

(ii) Distinctive function of the claims compared with the description

6–25   The description and the claims of a patent application have different functions. The primary function of the description is to enable a person skilled in the art thereafter to be able to carry out the invention. The primary function of the claims is to define the matter for which protection is sought in terms of the technical features of the invention (see Rule 29 EPC): thereafter the actual protection (*i.e.* the monopoly) given by a granted patent in each designated State is determined in accordance with Article 69 EPC by reference to the claims, ultimately by the courts of such States.[29]

(iii) Two-part claims

6–26   Rule 29(1) EPC requires that a claim should "where appropriate" contain two parts: (a) the preamble or pre-characterising portion and (b) the characterising portion. The first part should contain those technical features "which are necessary for the definition of the claimed subject matter, but which, in combination, are part of the prior art." The second part should contain the technical features "which, in combination . . . , it is desired to protect."

A two-part claim is not always appropriate. A one-part claim is preferable to the two-part claim provided for in Rule 29(1) EPC if the subject matter for which protection is sought is thereby defined clearly and concisely by avoiding inappropiate and complex formulations. However, it is then necessary to include in the description the information indicated in Rule 29(1)(a) EPC.[30]

---

[28] G2/88 O.J. EPO 1990, 93.
[29] T133/85 O.J. EPO 1988, 441.
[30] T170/84 O.J. EPO 1986, 400.

(b) Special kinds of claim

Each invention which is the subject of a European patent application **6–27** should be defined in the claim in accordance with its nature and subject matter.

There are basically two different types of claim, namely a claim to a physical entity (*e.g.* product, apparatus) and a claim to a physical activity (*e.g.* method, process, use). These two basic types of claim are sometimes referred to as the two possible "categories" of claim.

Within the above two basic types of claim various sub-classes are possible (*e.g.* a compound, a composition, a machine; or a manufacturing method, a process of producing a compound, a method of testing, etc.). Furthermore, claims including both features relating to physical activities and features relating to physical entities are also possible. There are no rigid lines of demarcation between the various possible forms of claim.

The technical features of a claim to a physical entity are the physical parameters of the entity, and the technical features of a claim to an activity are the physical steps which define such activity.[31]

The protection available under the EPC for certain specific kinds of invention is dependent to a large extent upon an appropriate choice of form and wording for the claims. Some particular kinds of claim are considered below.

(i) Use claims

The possibility that a European patent application may include use **6–28** claims is clearly recognised in the EPC (see, for example, Rules 29(2) and 30 EPC).

The recognition or discovery of a previously unknown property of a known compound, such property providing a new technical effect, can clearly involve a valuable and inventive contribution to the art.[32]

(ii) Functional claims

The inclusion of functional features in claims is permissible in European **6–29** patent applications and patents in certain circumstances, as discussed below. Clearly such claims can provide a broad extent of protection.

The allowability of functional claims is an aspect of claim definition and is primarily governed by the requirements of Article 84 EPC–not only that of clarity, but also that of support by the description. Furthermore, questions of sufficiency of description under Article 83 EPC may also arise.

Rule 29(1) EPC prescribes that the definition of a claimed invention shall be "in terms of (its) technical features." A technical feature may be a functional feature, that is, a limitation by result. The limitation may be with respect to either a physical entity or a physical activity.

---

[31] G2/88 O.J. EPO 1990, 3.
[32] *Ibid.*

The extent to which a claim may include functional features is clearly related partly to the nature of the claimed invention and partly to the appropriate extent of protection which can properly be conferred upon it. It is generally recognised that a claim which defines an invention almost entirely in terms of functional features by covering all methods of achieving a desired result is not normally allowable. Where the line is drawn in allowing functional features in a particular case would seem to depend upon finding a proper balance between an appropriately wide protection for the patentee and sufficient legal certainty for competitors as to what is inside and what is outside the extent of protection conferred. Furthermore, functional claims commonly require an especially detailed description of how to carry out the claimed invention so as to allow what is claimed to be achieved without undue burden.

Functional features defining a technical result are permissible in a claim if, from an objective viewpoint, such features cannot otherwise be defined more precisely without restricting the scope of the invention, and if these features provide instructions which are sufficiently clear for the expert to reduce them to practice without undue burden, if necessary with reasonable experiments.[33]

In some cases, it is only possible to define the invention in a way which gives a fair protection having regard to the nature of the invention which has been described, by using functional terminology in the claims.[34]

(c) Prescribed requirements for claims

6–30   Article 84 EPC requires that the claims shall be:

(a) clear and concise ("clarity");
(b) supported by the description ("support").

These distinct requirements are considered separately in sections (d) and (e) below. Such requirements must be fulfilled if a European patent is to be granted, and objections to grant during examination of an application will arise if they are not fulfilled. However, objections to a European patent after grant may not be based on these requirements – see paragraphs 3–19 above.

(d) Clarity

(i) Self-sufficiency of claims

6–31   As a general principle, the claims should be self-sufficient in themselves. As stated in Rule 29(6) EPC, "Claims shall not, except where absolutely necessary, rely, in respect of technical features of the invention, on references to the description or drawings."

Internal consistency. The claims, *per se*, must be free of contradiction: it must be possible to understand them without reference to the description,

---

[33] T68/85 O.J. EPO 1987, 228.
[34] T292/85 O.J. EPO 1989, 275.

especially as the description is not translated into all the official languages (Article 14(7) EPC).[35]

"Omnibus" claims containing direct references to the description. Claims relying on references to the description in the specification in respect of all their technical features are disallowable as contrary to Rules 29(4) and 29(6) EPC, unless absolutely necessary, *e.g.* when a plurality of conditions would not lend themselves to verbal expression without such a reference. The onus is on the applicant to show such exceptionality.[36]

Reference to the description for interpretation. Nevertheless, it is clear from Article 69 EPC that reference can and should properly be made to the description in order to interpret the claims, and thus to understand the extent of protection sought.

(ii) Specific cases concerning clarity

Specific circumstances concerning questions of clarity of claims are considered below. 6–32

Constituents of a mixture. In a claim for a mixture, the proportions give for each constituent must add up to the requisite total (100% in the case of percentages) for each composition claimed.[37]

Parameters in claims. Article 84 EPC may be fulfilled in a claim to a product when the characteristics of the product are specified by parameters related to the physical structure of the product, provided that those parameters can be clearly and reliably determined by objective procedures which are usual in the art.[38]

Reference signs in claims. The purpose of reference signs in a claim (Rule 29(7) EPC) is to make the claims easier to understand. They do not limit the scope of the claim but they do affect its clarity and may enable it to be expressed more concisely than would otherwise be possible.[39]

Chemical formulae in appendix to claims. The setting out of such structural formulae in an appendix to the claims is contrary to Rule 29(6) EPC, which provides that claims shall not, except where absolutely necessary, rely, in respect of the technical features of the invention, on references to the description or drawings.[40]

Product-by-process claims. A claim to a product which is defined in terms of the process for its preparation is allowable having regard to Article 84 EPC only if the product itself fulfils the requirements for patentability (Articles 52 to 57 EPC), and if there is no other information

---

[35] T2/80 O.J. EPO 1981, 431.
[36] T150/82 O.J. EPO 1984, 309.
[37] T2/80 O.J. EPO 1981, 431.
[38] T94/82 O.J. EPO 1984, 75.
[39] T237/84 O.J. EPO 1987, 309.
[40] T271/88 June 6, 1989.

available in the application which could enable the applicant to define the product satisfactorily by reference to its composition, structure or some other testable parameter. This in order to minimise uncertainty.[41]

Inclusion of essential features. Article 84 EPC requires amongst other things that the claims, which define the matter for which protection is sought (*i.e.* the object of the invention as implied by Article 52(1) EPC), be clear. This has to be interpreted as meaning not only that a claim from a technical point of view must be comprehensible, but also that it must define clearly the object of the invention, that is to say, indicate all the essential features thereof.

All essential features have to be regarded as features which are necessary to obtain the desired effect or, differently expressed, which are necessary to solve the technical problem with which the application is concerned.[42]

This view of the first part of Article 84 EPC is complementary to the requirement of support by the description in the second sentence of Article 84 EPC, considered below.

(e) Support by the description

6–33   This requirement of Article 84 EPC defines the relationship between the description (including any drawings) and the claims of a European patent application. In the case of inventions concerning micro-organisms, the information derived from a deposited micro-organism in accordance with Rule 28 EPC supplements that of the description *per se* (see paragraphs 6–15 *et seq.* above).

Since most claims are generalisations of examples disclosed in the description, the purpose of Article 84 EPC must be seen as safe-guarding that the claims do not cover any subject matter which, after reading the description, would not be at the disposal of the skilled person.[43]

It follows that the extent of the description ultimately governs the matter for which protection may be sought in the claims. The requirement for support by the description also effectively determines the permissible width of the claims (in combination with the prior art). In general terms, the subject matter of an invention as defined in the claims cannot be wider than the subject matter of the invention which has been disclosed in the description. Nevertheless, generalisation in the claims of the subject matter disclosed in the description is clearly permissible, in order to ensure that an appropriate extent of protection can be derived from the claims. The extent of protection defined by the claims should correspond to and be justified by, the actual technical contribution to the art which has been disclosed in the description.[44]

---

[41] T150/82 O.J. EPO 1984, 309.
[42] T32/82 O.J. EPO 1984, 354.
[43] T26/81 O.J. EPO 1982, 211.
[44] T409/91 O.J. EPO 1994, 653.

7. Amendment of the Specification

CONTENTS

A. Introduction

7–01   The possibility of amending the description, claims and drawings of a patent application or patent, both after filing and after grant, is a matter of a great practical importance. The description and claims of an application are commonly originally drafted without full knowledge either of all the prior art which may be used later to challenge its validity, or of all the ways in which the invention may be carried out. The wording of an application as originally drafted may not be as clear as it could be, especially since the draftsman is under pressure to file the application quickly. The information in an application as filed relating to the ways in which the invention can be carried out may not be as complete as it could be. In many circumstances, amendment offers the only possibility of curing invalidity, having regard to previously unknown prior art, for example, or of ensuring that the claims confer legal protection which corresponds to what has been invented and which is of commercial value.

Nevertheless, primarily in the interest of legal certainty, the extent to which amendments are possible, whether after filing of an application or after the grant of a patent is clearly restricted. Such legal certainty is especially important having regard to the early publication of European patent applications (see paragraph 1–03).

The relevant law as to the allowability of amendments and corrections to an application or patent is governed by Article 123 EPC and Rules 86 to 88 EPC. The procedural aspects of amendment in proceedings before the Examining Division (i.e. pre-grant) and before the Opposition Division (i.e. post-grant) are considered above in paragraphs 2–11 et seq., and 3–28 et seq., respectively. The substantive aspects of amendment (i.e. amendment to the description, claims or drawings) in proceedings before the EPO are considered below under the following headings:

(a) Amendments after filing: Article 123(2) EPC;
(b) Amendments after grant: Article 123(3) EPC;
(c) Corrections after filing: Rule 88 EPC;

The possibility of such amendment after grant in national proceedings is not governed by Articles 123(2) and (3) EPC, as such, but by provisions in national laws (which may or may not correspond exactly with the provisions of Article 123 EPC).

In fact, the wording of Article 123(2) EPC is appropriate to cover the whole of the subsequent life of an application or patent, both in proceedings before the EPO and before national courts, and amounts to a general principle for such applications and patents. The wording of Article 123(3) EPC is specific to "opposition proceedings" before the EPO, however, and makes room for the possibility of other provisions as to allowability of amendments in national proceedings.

B. AMENDMENTS AFTER FILING: FORMAL ASPECTS

(a) Introduction

The question to be considered in determining the allowability of any 7–02
amendment is whether the amended application or patent "contains
subject matter which extends beyond the content of the application as
filed". This applies to any amendment proposed after the initial filing of a
European patent application, and, therefore, applies in both pre-grant and
in post-grant (*i.e.* opposition) proceedings before the EPO.

Furthermore, the same consideration applies in relation to the
allowability of the filing of a divisional application (see paragraph 2–16),
since the same wording is common to Article 123(2) EPC and Article 76(1)
EPC.

(b) Constituents of "the application is filed"

Article 80 EPC provides that the date of filing shall be the date on which 7–03
documents filed by an applicant contain:

(a) an indication that a European patent is sought;
(b) the designation of at least one Contracting State;
(c) information identifying the applicant;
(d) a description and one or more claims.

(a), (b) and (c) are formal in nature.

The documents may also include other material, such as drawings and
an abstract, properly forming part of the application for some purposes.

(c) Documents not part of "the application as filed", for the purposes of Article 123(2) EPC

(i) The abstract

Although Article 78 EPC defines the requirements of a European patent 7–04
application as including an abstract (in addition to a description, one or
more claims, and any drawings referred to therein), it is made clear in
Article 85 EPC that even if an abstract has been filed on the allocated date
of filing, nevertheless it "shall merely serve as technical information; it
may not be taken into account for any other purpose . . .". Thus, for the
purpose of Article 123(2) EPC the content of the application as filed does
not include the abstract.[1]

(ii) Priority documents

For the purpose of Article 123(2) EPC the content of the application as 7–05
filed does not include any priority documents, even if they were filed on
the same day as the European patent application.[2]

---

[1] T407/86 [1988] EPOR 254; T246/86 O.J. EPO 1989, 199.
[2] T260/85 O.J. EPO 1989, 105.

(iii) Cross-referenced documents

7–06   The contents of a document to which reference is made in the description of the application as filed are prima facie not within "the content of the application as filed" for the purpose of Article 123(2) EPC.[3]

The conditions under which an amendment to the claims may be based upon the contents of such a cross-referenced document are discussed in paragraph 7–12 below.

C. AMENDMENTS AFTER FILING: SUBSTANTIVE PROVISIONS

(a) Basic principles

(i) Nature of the novelty test

7–07   The test for compliance with Article 123(2) EPC is basically a novelty test, *i.e.* no new subject matter must be generated by the amendment.[4] However, care is necessary when applying the law relating to novelty to consideration of proposed amendments, since it is the words of Article 123(2) EPC which must ultimately always be considered in each particular case.[5] In particular, the test for additional subject matter corresponds to the test for novelty only insofar as both require assessment of whether or not information is directly and unambiguously derivable from that previously presented, in the originally filed application or in a prior document respectively. It follows that an amendment is not allowable if the resulting change in content of the application, in other words the subject matter generated by the amendment, is novel when compared with the content of the original application or, looked at another way, if the said change in content would be novelty-destroying for a hypothetical future claim when the original content would not be. It is important that it is the change in content which is tested, that is, the amended content minus the original content, so that the test is applicable also to amendment by generalisation or omission of a feature.[6]

(ii) The content of the application: total information content

The content of the application means the total information content of the disclosure. This includes the original statements as to the problem to be solved.[7]

(b) Claim broadening before grant

(i) When permissible

7–08   If a technical feature is deleted from a claim in order not to exclude from protection certain embodiments of the invention, the broadening of the claim does not contravene Article 123(2) EPC as long as there is a

---

[3] T689/90 O.J. EPO 1993, 616.
[4] T201/83 O.J. EPO 1984, 481.
[5] T133/85 O.J. EPO 1988, 441.
[6] T194/84 O.J. EPO 1990, 59.
[7] T514/88 O.J. EPO 1992, 570.

basic for a claim lacking this feature in the application as filed. It is immaterial whether or not the feature in question is relevant to the inventive concept of the claimed subject matter.[8]

Thus, during examination of an application, it is possible without contravening Article 123(2) EPC to broaden a claim (*i.e.* to extend the protection conferred by it) provided that the subject matter which is within the claims for the first time as a result of the amendment was already part of the content of the original application as filed. The extent of a generic disclosure in the application as filed may depend upon what, in the context, the skilled reader would seriously contemplate as a possible practical embodiment of the described invention.[9]

Furthermore, the deletion of a feature in a claim is admissible if the sole purpose of such deletion is to clarify and/or resolve an inconsistency.[10]

(ii) Deletion of an essential feature not allowable

It is not permissible to delete from an independent claim a feature which 7–09 the application as originally filed consistently presents as being an essential feature of the invention,[11] because in such a case the application as filed contains no disclosure of the claimed invention without such feature.

(iii) What constitutes an essential/inessential feature?

The replacement or removal of a feature from a claim may not violate 7–10 Article 123(3) EPC provided the skilled person would directly and unambiguously recognise that

(1) the feature was not explained as essential in the disclosure,
(2) it is not, as such, indispensable for the function of the invention in the light of the technical problem it serves to solve, and
(3) the replacement or removal requires no real modification of other features to compensate for the change. The feature in question may be inessential even if it was incidentally but consistently presented in combination with other features of the invention.[12]

(iv) Generalisation of a claimed feature

The allowability of an amendment by which a particular feature in a 7–11 claim is generalised depends upon the application of the principles discussed above.

Thus, replacing a disclosed specific feature by a broad general expression is not allowable under Article 123(2) EPC where use of such a general expression for the first time explicitly associates with the subject matter of the application specific features going beyond the initial disclosure.[13]

---

[8] T66/85 O.J. EPO 1989, 167.
[9] T187/91 O.J. EPO 1994, 572.
[10] T172/82 O.J. EPO 1983, 493.
[11] T260/85 O.J. EPO 1989, 105.
[12] T331/87 O.J. EPO 1991, 22.
[13] T416/86 O.J. EPO 1989, 308.

Similarly, in a particular case[14] a generalisation of the term "sealing bead" into the term "pressure seals" in the main claim of a divisional application was refused on the basis that an amendment is not allowable if the subject matter generated by it is novel. It was held that the term "pressure seals" includes all the equivalents of the disclosed specific "sealing beads" into the content of the application, that is, subject matter which is novel with regard to the application as filed.

(c) Claim narrowing

(i) Addition of a feature to a claim

7–12　The addition of a feature to a claim will narrow the protection sought. However, such an addition is not allowable under Article 123(2) EPC if it causes the subject matter of the application to be extended beyond the content of the application as filed.

For example, if the particular feature which is proposed to be added to a claim is a component which has only been disclosed in the application as filed in association with another component, and there is nothing in the application as filed to indicate that the invention could consist of a device having the first such component but not the other component, the amendment will not be allowable.[15] On the other hand, even if the proposed additional feature is a component which has only been described in the application as filed in association with other components, the amendment will be allowable provided that it is evident to a skilled reader of the application as filed that the combination of features in the amended claim produces the result sought in the application, and is therefore a disclosed embodiment of the invention.[16]

Particular problems arise if the feature which is proposed to be added to a claim has not been disclosed in the description as such, but has only been disclosed in a cross-referenced document identified in the description.

In one case, a particular catalyst which was the subject of the claimed invention was further characterised as to its parameters in a cross-referenced document. The addition of characterising parameters to the claim which had previously only been disclosed in the cross-referenced document was allowed, since such parameters were features which unequivocally formed part of the invention for which protection was sought.[17]

However, the addition of further technical features to a claim, which features have only been disclosed in a cross-referenced document, is only allowable if the description leaves no doubt:

(i) that protection is or may be sought for such features;
(ii) that such features contribute to the technical aim of the invention; and implicitly belong to the description of the invention;

---

[14] T265/88 O.J. [1990] EPOR 399.
[15] T54/82 O.J. EPO 1983, 446.
[16] T17/86 O.J. EPO 1989, 297.
[17] T6/84 O.J. EPO 1985, 238.

(iii) that such features are precisely defined and identifiable.[18]

(ii) Disclaimers

Substraction of embodiments. An amendment by way of a disclaimer in a **7–13**
claim in the form of a statement in the claim whose effect is to subtract
certain specified embodiments from the more general definition of the
scope of the claim is allowable, if the subject matter remaining in the claim
cannot be defined more clearly and concisely directly, *i.e.* by positive
features.[19]

**Delimitation with respect to prior art or insufficiency: no basis for the
exclusion necessary.** In cases where what is claimed in general overlaps
with the state of the art, it is permissible to exclude a certain state of the
art from the claimed invention by means of a disclaimer, even if the
original documents give no specific basis for such an exclusion.

Such a disclaimer is justified because the inventive teaching originally
disclosed in the application is not changed as a whole merely by delimiting
it with respect to the state of the art or with respect to what has proved
not to be functional.[20]

Delimitation to provide an inventive step: a basis necessary. It is not
allowable to give inventive quality to an obvious teaching by subsequently
adding a feature which was not originally specifically disclosed, because
the technical teaching contained in the original documents would thereby
be substantially modified.[21]

Disclaimers from ranges: subject to novelty of what remains. In relation
to a claimed invention which includes a parameter defined in terms of a
range of values, if the prior art discloses individual examples having
individual values of such parameters in combination with the other
claimed features, a specific disclaimer of such individual examples is not
normally permissible, if a skilled person would not regard the teaching of
individual examples as absolutely limited to the individual values associated with such examples, because in such circumstances the disclaimer is
not effective to avoid loss of novelty.[22]

(d) Clarification of a claim

An amendment to a claim to clarify an inconsistency does not con- **7–14**
travene Article 123(2) EPC if the amended claim has the same meaning as
the unamended claim on its true construction in the context of the
specification.[23]

---

[18] T689/90 O.J. EPO 1993, 616.
[19] T4/80 O.J. EPO 1982, 149.
[20] T4/80 O.J. EPO 1982, 149; T433/86 (1988) EPOR 97; T170/87 O.J. EPO 1989, 441.
[21] T170/87 O.J. EPO 1989, 441.
[22] T188/83 O.J. EPO 1984, 555; T290/86 O.J. EPO 1992, 414.
[23] T271/84 O.J. EPO 1987, 405.

(e) Amendment of an erroneous technical calculation

7–15   Correction of an erroneous technical calculation in a claim is allowable under Article 123(2) EPC if the amendment would be regarded by the skilled reader as clearly implied by the disclosure of the application as filed. If more than one arithmetic possibility of correction can be envisaged, the correction chosen must be the one which the application as a whole clearly implies.[24]

(f) Change in position of a feature in a claim

7–16   If a change in the position of a feature within a claim does not alter its meaning (*e.g.* placing a feature within the preamble instead of within the characterising portion of the claim), the extent of protection conferred remains unchanged and such an amendment does not contravene Article 123(2) EPC.[25]

(g) Amendments to the description

(i) Addition of reference to prior art

7–17   The mere addition to the description of a reference to prior art does not contravene Article 123(2) EPC. Even the addition of a discussion of the advantages of the invention with reference to such prior art may be allowable, depending on the actual language used and the circumstances of the case.[26]

(ii) Clarification and additional explanation

7–18   If a technical feature is disclosed in the application as filed, and its technical effect is not mentioned in the application as filed but can be deduced from such application using the common general knowledge of the skilled person in the art, subsequent clarification of that effect in the description does not contravene Article 123(2) EPC.[27]

(h) Relationship between Article 123(2) EPC and Article 84 EPC

7–19   Article 84 EPC, in particular insofar as it requires the claims to be "supported by" the description, must be satisfied by every application, whether or not amendments have been proposed. Article 123(2) EPC is only concerned with the allowability of proposed amendments.

    If an amendment to an application (either the description or the claims) is proposed, the application must be examined to ensure that the require-

---

[24] T13/83 O.J. EPO 1984, 428.
[25] T16/86 February 4, 1988.
[26] T11/82 O.J. EPO 1983, 479.
[27] T37/82 O.J. EPO 1984, 71.

ments of both Article 123(2) EPC and Article 84 EPC are met. The requirement of Article 123(2) EPC is clearly different from the requirement of Article 84 EPC, both at a matter of wording and as a matter of substance.

D. AMENDMENTS AFTER GRANT

(a) Introduction

Article 123(2) EPC provides that during opposition proceedings before 7–20 the EPO "the claims of the European patent may not be amended . . . in such a way as to extend the protection conferred." This provision is additional to that of Article 123(2) EPC. In opposition proceedings, therefore, both Article 123(2) and (3) EPC are applicable.

When interpreting Article 123 EPC in general, and Article 123(2) EPC in particular, it is important to consider also the provisions of Article 138 EPC, which provides the grounds for revocation of a European patent under national laws. In particular, Article 138(1)(c) and (d) EPC provide grounds of revocation of a European patent in proceedings before national courts which correspond to the requirements of Article 123(2) and (3) EPC. The extent of protection conferred by a European patent is determined in accordance with Article 69(1) EPC and its Protocol by the terms of the claims but also by reference to the description and drawings.

Once a European patent has been granted, an act by a third party which would not infringe the patent as granted should not be able to become an infringing act as a result of amendment after grant. This is the essential purpose of Article 123(2) EPC.

As discussed in paragraphs 7–06 *et seq.* above, when considering Article 123(2) EPC the question of extension of subject matter depends upon a comparison with the "application as filed". When considering Article 123(3) EPC, however, the question of extension of protection depends upon a comparison with the claims as granted.

(b) Basic principles

The protection conferred by a European patent is determined in 7–21 accordance with Article 69(1) EPC by the terms of the claims, and the description and drawings are to be used for the purpose of interpreting the claims.

When considering whether a proposed amendment to the claims is such as to extend the protection conferred, the first step is to determine the extent of protection which is conferred by the patent before the amendment. The question then to be considered is whether the subject matter defined by the claims is more or less narrowly defined as a result of the amendment.

The subject matter of a claimed invention involves two aspects: first, the category of the claim, and secondly, the technical features, which contribute to its technical subject matter.

As explained in paragraph 6–27, the word "category" is used to distinguish between, for example, a "compound" or "composition" claim, on the one hand (*i.e.* a physical entity), and a "use" claim or a "process" claim, on the other hand (*i.e.* a physical activity).

A proposed amendment may involve a change of category, or a change in the technical features of the invention, or both. Each type of amendment requires separate consideration.

(c) Change of category

7–22   An amendment by way of change of category is only exceptionally allowable under Article 123(2) EPC.[28] Each possible individual change of category has to be considered against the requirement that the protection conferred by the claim cannot be extended by the change of category. The allowability of some possible changes of category (*e.g.* "composition" to "method of preparing the composition") is not easy to decide.

(i) "Product" to "use"

The protection conferred by a claim to a physical entity, *i.e.* a product such as a chemical compound, *per se*, is absolute, and extends to that compound wherever it exists and whatever its context. It follows that a claim to a particular use of a product is in effect a claim to the compound only when it is being used in the course of the particular physical activity (the use). Such a claim therefore confers less protection than a claim to the product.

Thus, an amendment of granted claims directed to a product so that the amended claims are directed to the use of that product for a particular purpose, is not open to objection under Article 123(3) EPC.[29]

(ii) "Method of working" to "apparatus" for such a method

In one case,[30] it was held that a skilled person could readily deduce the apparatus suitable for carrying out the protected process from the technical teaching defined in the patent, and that the extent of protection conferred by the granted process patent thus also encompassed the apparatus for carrying out the protected process. The amendment was, therefore, allowed.

(d) Change of technical features

7–23   In such a case, if the technical features of the claimed invention after amendment are more narrowly defined, the extent of the protection conferred is less; and if such technical features are less narrowly defined as

---

[28] T378/86 O.J. EPO 1988, 386.
[29] G2/88 O.J. EPO 1990, 93.
[30] T378/86 O.J. EPO 1988, 386.

a result of amendment, the protection conferred is therefore extended. Clearly, if technical features are changed by an amendment, in that the technical subject matter of the claims after amendment is outside the scope of the technical subject matter before amendment, there is then necessarily an extension of protection.[31]

(e) Clarification of a claimed feature

Amendment of a claim to clarify an inconsistency does not contravene   **7–24** Article 123(3) EPC if the amended claim has the same meaning as the unamended claim.[32]

(f) Conflict between Article 123(2) EPC and Article 123(3) EPC

In some cases, a claim of an application has been amended before grant   **7–25** by the addition of a technical feature with the approval of the Examining Division, no objection being taken under Article 123(2) EPC.

Subsequently, in opposition proceedings, if an Opposition Division or Board of Appeal decides under Article 100(c) EPC that the addition of such feature before grant caused the subject matter of the European patent to extend beyond the content of the application as filed, and was therefore contrary to Article 123(2) EPC, it is not possible to maintain the patent unamended because the ground of opposition in Article 100(c) EPC prejudices maintenance of the patent with such text. Furthermore, amendment of the patent by deletion of the feature which was added to the claim before grant would be contrary to Article 123(3) EPC, and is therefore also not possible.[33] Such a patent can consequently only be maintained if there is a basis in the application as filed for replacing such feature without violating Article 123(3) EPC.[34]

E. CORRECTION OF AN OBVIOUS MISTAKE IN THE DESCRIPTION, CLAIMS OR DRAWINGS

(a) Introduction

A mistake in any document filed at the EPO may be corrected on   **7–26** request. However, if the request for such correction concerns a description, claims or drawings, the correction must be obvious in the sense that it is immediately evident that nothing else would have been intended than what is offered as the correction.

Thus, for a correction under Rule 88 EPC, second sentence, to be allowable, two matters must be established:

---

[31] G2/88 O.J. EPO 1990, 93.
[32] T271/84 O.J. EPO 1987, 405.
[33] G1/93 O.J. EPO 1994, 541.
[34] T231/89 O.J. EPO 1993, 13; T108/91 O.J. EPO 1994, 228.

(i) that there is a mistake in the description, claims or drawings;

(ii) that both the mistake and its correction are obvious in the above sense.

Furthermore, correction of an error under Rule 88 EPC is discretionary.[35]

Insofar as Rule 88 EPC, first sentence not only concerns corrections to a description, claims or drawings, but also allows corrections to any other document filed at the EPO, a number of decisions specifically concerning corrections to other such documents also set out principles which are applicable to corrections in a description, claims or drawings.

The correction of mistakes in documents other than a description, claims or drawings which have been filed at the EPO is considered separately in paragraphs 5–01 *et seq.*

(b) Declaratory effect of a correction under Rule 88 EPC

7–27   The correction of a mistake restores the application to the form in which it has been established that the applicant intended to file it, and is declaratory of the content of the application as filed.[36]

(c) Relationship with Article 123(2) EPC

7–28   A correction of the description, claims or drawings under Rule 88 EPC is a special case of an amendment under Article 123 EPC. Such a correction is only allowable within the limits of what a skilled person would derive from these documents as filed, using common general knowledge and seen objectively and relative to the date of filing. Since such a correction merely expresses what a skilled person using common general knowledge would already derive from the application as filed, and as stated above is declaratory in nature, it will not contravene Article 123(2) EPC.[37]

(d) Existence of a mistake

7–29   For the purpose of Rule 88 EPC, a mistake may be said to exist if the document does not express the true intention of the person on whose behalf it was filed. The mistake may take the form of an incorrect statement or it may result from an omission.[38]

In order to establish that a correction should be allowed, the burden is on the applicant to establish that a mistake has been made and what the mistake was. It is the responsibility of the person requesting correction to put evidence as to the relevant facts fully and frankly before the EPO. Rule 88 EPC may not be used to enable a person to give effect to a change of his mind or a subsequent development of his plans.[39]

---

[35] T200/89 O.J. EPO 1992, 46.
[36] J4/85, O.J. EPO 1986, 205; G3/89, G11/91 O.J. EPO 1993, 117 and 125.
[37] G3/89, G11/91 O.J. EPO 1993, 117 and 125.
[38] J4/85 O.J. EPO 1986, 205; J8/80 O.J. EPO 1980, 293; J6/91 O.J. EPO 1994, 349.
[39] J8/80 O.J. EPO 1980, 293.

In order to establish the existence of a mistake or error in a document filed at the EPO, which is a subjective matter, reference may be made to any relevant documents or other evidence, including in appropriate cases the file history,[40] or a priority document whether or not filed with the application as filed.[41]

(e) Obviousness of the mistake and its correction

Correction of a mistake in the description, claims or drawings is only 7–30 allowable under Rule 88 EPC second sentence, if such documents contain such an obvious error that a skilled person is in no doubt that the information in such documents is not correct, and cannot be meant to read as such, using common general knowledge. Furthermore, it must be obvious to the skilled person what the correction should be. Thus, the skilled person must be able to ascertain unequivocally the information that should have been stated. Evidence of what was common general knowledge on the date of filing may be furnished in any suitable form.[42]

If it is doubtful to the skilled reader whether any information in such documents as filed is incorrect, or it is doubtful what the correction should be, a correction under Rule 88 EPC is not allowable.[43]

(f) Mistakes concerning drawings

According to Rule 43 EPC, if upon examination of a European patent 7–31 application it is found that the drawings of the application are missing or were filed late, then in the former case they may be filed within one month, and in either case the date of filing of the application becomes the date on which the drawings were filed (and if they are not filed in due time any reference to them in the application has to be deleted).

A mistake in relation to the drawings of an application, whether by way of incorrect content or omission, may in principle be corrected under Rule 88 EPC; and if so corrected, Rule 43 EPC is not applicable, in view of the declaratory nature of such a correction,[44] so that no loss of priority results.

A missing part of a drawing, such as a missing figure, is not considered as a missing drawing for the purpose of Rule 43 EPC, and is correctable under Rule 88 EPC,[45] again with no loss of priority.

(g) No estoppel from correction following approval of text

If, following approval of the text of a patent just before grant under 7–32 Rule 51(4) EPC, the proprietor discovers an error in the text of the patent as granted, he is not estopped from correcting the error under Rule 88 EPC.[46]

---

[40] T200/89 O.J. EPO 1992, 46.
[41] J4/85 O.J. EPO 1986, 205.
[42] G3/89, G11/91 O.J. EPO 1993, 117 and 125.
[43] *ibid.*
[44] J4/85 O.J. EPO 1986, 205 (overruling J1/82 O.J. EPO 1982, 293); G3/89, G11/91 O.J. EPO 1993, 117 and 125.
[45] J19/80 O.J. EPO 1981, 65.
[46] T200/89 O.J. EPO 1992, 246.

8. Patentable Subject-Matter

CONTENTS

A. INTRODUCTION

(a) Positive requirements for patentability

Article 52(1) EPC sets out four criteria which must be met if a European **8–01** patent application is to be granted:

(a) there must be an invention;
(b) the invention must be susceptible of industrial application;
(c) the invention must be new;
(d) the invention must involve an inventive step.

Requirement (a) is concerned with the subject matter of the application, and together with requirement (b), is considered in the present chapter. Requirements (c) and (d), novelty and inventive step, are considered separately in Chapters 10 and 11.

If the above four criteria are met, the wording of Article 52(1) EPC is mandatory: European patents "shall be granted" for such inventions.

(b) Exclusions and exceptions from patentability

Articles 52 and 53 EPC identify various types of subject matter which **8–02** are not patentable under the EPC, either by way of exclusion (Article 52 EPC) or by way of exception (Article 53 EPC). In each case the effect is the same, *i.e.* the subject matter is not patentable.

(i) Article 52 EPC: exclusions

The scheme of Article 52 EPC is to set out in paragraphs (2) and (3) **8–03** certain categories of subject matter–the "mathematical" exclusions–which are not to be regarded as "inventions" (requirement (a) above), and to set out in paragraph (4) further categories of subject matter–the "medical" exclusions–which are not to be regarded as "inventions which are suscept-ible of industrial application" (requirement (b) above). All such categories of subject matter are, therefore, excluded from patentability as a matter of definition.

The difference in wording between paragraphs (2) and (4) results from the nature of the subject matters that are being excluded from patentability in the respective paragraphs. The subject matters which are set out in paragraph (2) are excluded primarily because they have traditionally been regarded within national patent laws as more in the nature of ideas than industrial manufactures. In contrast, the methods which are set out in paragraph (4) are excluded from patentability, even though such methods are capable of being applied industrially, as a matter of policy. Thus, the wording of paragraph (4) is implicitly recognizing that such methods are susceptible of industrial application as a matter of reality, but provides that they "shall not be regarded as inventions which are susceptible of industrial application," by way of legal fiction.[1]

---

[1] T116/85 O.J. EPO 1989, 13.

Discoveries, mathematical methods, computer programs, etc. Article 52(2) EPC excludes:

"in particular:

(a) discoveries, scientific theories and mathematical methods;
(b) aesthetic creations;
(c) schemes, rules and methods for performing mental acts, playing games or doing business, and programs for computers;
(d) presentations of information."

The above exclusions are subject to the important qualification set out in Article 52(3) EPC, namely that such subject matter and activities are excluded from patentability "only to the extent to which a European patent application or patent relates to such subject matter or activities **as such**" (emphasis added).

Methods of medical treatment, diagnostic methods. Article 52(4) EPC excludes:

"Methods for treatment of the human or animal body by

(a) surgery, or
(b) therapy;

Diagnostic methods practised on the human or animal body."

The above exclusions are stated not to apply "to products, in particular substances or compositions, for use in any of these methods." Only inventions claimed in terms of methods are excluded.

(ii) Article 53 EPC: exceptions

8–04   Article 53 EPC defines certain types of invention–the "morality" and "biological" exceptions–which by their nature cannot be the subject of a granted European patent. The exceptions to patentability under Article 53 EPC may meet all of the requirements for patentability set out in Article 52 EPC, both in fact and by way of definition, but are not patentable for reasons which are essentially based on public policy.

Inventions contrary to "ordre public" or morality. Article 53(a) EPC excepts from patentability "Inventions the publication or exploitation of which would be contrary to 'ordre public' or morality."

This is subject to the qualification that the "exploitation shall not be deemed to be so contrary merely because it is prohibited by law or regulation in some or all of the Contracting States."

Biological matter. Article 53(b) EPC excepts from patentability: "Plant or animal varieties; essentially biological processes for the production of plants or animals." The latter exception is subject to the qualification that it does not apply to "micro-biological processes or the products thereof."

B. DISCOVERIES, MATHEMATICAL METHODS, COMPUTER PROGRAMS, ETC: EXCLUSIONS UNDER ARTICLE 52(2) AND (3) EPC

(a) The nature of these exclusions

(i) Abstract compared to technical character

The concept of a patentable "invention" has always been notoriously 8–05 difficult to define, and the EPC does not make any attempt to do so. Article 52(2) EPC simply defines a list of particular categories of subject matter which are not within the concept of an "invention." It follows from the presence of the words "in particular" in Article 52(2) EPC that such subject matter is not a complete definition of what is excluded. Subject matter which is similar in nature to the defined categories could also be excluded. Thus, the exclusion may be generalised to subject matter which is essentially abstract in character, which is non-physical and, therefore, is not characterised by technical features in the sense of Rule 29(1) EPC.[2]

The excluded categories in Article 52(2)(a) to (d) EPC have in common that they refer to activities which do not aim at any direct technical result but are rather of an abstract and intellectual character. To be patentable, claimed subject matter must have a technical character and thus, in principle, be industrially applicable. In other words, it must provide a technical contribution to the art.[3]

(ii) Consideration of the claimed invention as a whole

When considering patentability it is necessary to consider the claimed invention as a whole. Decisive is what technical contribution the invention as defined in the claim, when considered as a whole, makes to the known art.[4]

If a claimed invention makes use of both technical and non-technical means, the use of non-technical means does not detract from the technical character of the overall teaching. The EPC does not ask that a patentable invention be exclusively or largely of a technical nature; in other words, it does not prohibit the patenting of inventions consisting of a mix of technical and non-technical elements.[5]

On the other hand, a claim which, when taken as a whole, does not have a technical character (for example, the claim defines essentially a business operation) is not patentable even though the claimed method includes steps which include a technical component. The true nature of the claimed subject matter remains the same, even though some technical means are used to perform it.[6]

(b) Excluded subject matter: examples

Objections to patentability under Article 52(2) EPC commonly fall under more than one of the categories set out in Article 52(2)(a) to (d) EPC. Thus, the headings below are merely illustrative.

---

[2] T163/85 O.J. EPO 1990, 379.
[3] T22/85 O.J. EPO 1990, 12; T854/90 O.J. EPO 1993, 669.
[4] T208/84 O.J. EPO 1987, 14.
[5] T26/86 O.J. EPO 1988, 19.
[6] T854/90 O.J. EPO 1993, 669.

(i) Computer-related inventions: mathematical methods

8–06   A clear distinction should be drawn between a mathematical method or algorithm as such, and its use in a technical process. A mathematical method or algorithm is carried out on numbers (whatever these numbers may represent) and provides a result also in numerical form, the mathematical method or algorithm being only an abstract concept prescribing how to operate on the numbers. No direct technical result is produced by the method as such. In contrast thereto, if a mathematical method is used in a technical process, that process is caried out on a physical entity (which may be a material object but equally an image stored as an electric signal) by some technical means implementing the method and provides as its result a certain change in that entity. The technical means might include a computer comprising suitable hardware or an appropriately programmed general purpose computer.

Therefore, even if the idea underlying an invention may be considered to reside in a mathematical method, a claim directed to a technical process in which the method is used does not seek protection for the mathematical method as such.

Similarly, a claim directed to a technical process which is carried out under the control of a program (whether by means of hardware or software), cannot be regarded as relating to a computer program as such.[7]

In deciding whether a claim relates to a computer program as such, it is not necessary to give a relative weighting to its technical and non-technical features. If the invention defined in the claim uses technical means, it can be patented provided it meets the requirements of Articles 52 to 57 EPC.[8]

A claim directed to an excluded activity but at the same time containing such technical features may be allowable. Thus, a contribution to the art within an excluded category of subject matter, when a defined in a claim as appied to technical means for carrying out a method, may provide patentable subject matter.[9] However, the mere setting out of the sequence of steps necessary to perform the activity in terms of functions or functional means to be realised with the aid of conventional computer hardware elements does not import any technical considerations. There is then no technical character in that activity or in the claimed subject matter considered as a whole.[10]

As regards computer-related and similar inventions, the relevant principles may be summarised as follows:

(1) A claim to a computer program is not patentable.
(2) A claim which includes features defining a computer program may or may not be patentable.
(3) To determine patentability, the claim as a whole must be considered so as to determine the nature of the technical contribution to the art.

---

[7] T208/84 O.J. EPO 1987, 14.
[8] T26/86 O.J. EPO 1988, 19.
[9] T38/86 O.J. EPO 1990, 384.
[10] T22/85 O.J. EPO 1990, 12.

(ii) Discovery compared with invention

The phrase "discovery as such" is commonly considered to mean the **8–07** mere recognition of what already exists. Thus, human intervention or interaction of a technical nature with what has been discovered may constitute a distinction between "discovery as such" and "invention."

When deciding whether a claimed invention is a discovery within the meaning of Article 52(2)(a) EPC, an essential first step in such consideration is to construe the claim so as to determine its technical features. If, after such determination, it is clear that the claimed invention relates to a discovery or other excluded subject matter "as such" (Article 52(3) EPC), then the exclusion of Article 52(2) EPC applies. The fact that the idea or concept underlying the claimed subject matter resides in a discovery does not necessarily mean that the claimed subject matter is a discovery "as such."[11]

(iii) Aesthetic creation/presentation of information

In one case[12] the claimed subject matter was a flexible plastic disc jacket **8–08** having a coloured outer surface (other than black). An advantage of resistance to marking with fingerprints was suggested. The claimed subject matter was held to be a purely aesthetic effect which contributed nothing technical.

The further claimed advantage of classification of the jackets according to colour was held to be "presentation of information."

In another case[13] the claimed invention was a colour television signal characterised by features of the transmitting and receiving system in which it was to be used, which were, therefore, technical in nature. A distinction was made between two kinds of information, namely the information transmitted per se, and information comprised by the technical features of the transmission system.

The claimed system was a physical reality which could be directly detected by technological means, and was technical rather than abstract in character, and, therefore, patentable.

C. MEDICAL TREATMENT AND DIAGNOSIS: EXCLUSIONS UNDER ARTICLE 52(4) EPC

(a) The nature of these exclusions

Methods for treatment of the human or animal body by surgery or **8–09** therapy and diagnostic methods practised on the human or animal body are not patentable.

---

[11] G2/88 O.J. EPO 1990, 93.
[12] T119/88 O.J. EPO 1990, 395.
[13] T163/85 O.J. EPO 1990, 379.

These exclusions only concern inventions claimed in terms of a method, as is emphasised by the final sentence of Article 52(4) EPC.

The policy behind the exclusion of such methods is in order to ensure that those who carry out such methods as part of the medical treatment of humans or the veterinary treatment of animals should not be inhibited by patents.[14]

Such policy is a compromise between the need to encourage research in relation to medical compositions and the need not to restrict the medical and veterinary treatments normally carried out by physicians.

The medical treatment of both human and animal bodies is excluded from patentability. Human beings and animals are treated equally in this respect.

(b) Veterinary treatment compared with agriculture: the relationship between Articles 52(4) and 57 EPC

8–10   Article 57 EPC defines and explains the nature of the requirement in Article 52(1) EPC that the subject matter is "susceptible of industrial application." In particular, this Article makes it quite clear that under the EPC, agriculture is a kind of industry; and that agricultural methods are therefore, in general, methods which are susceptible of industrial application.

However, the scheme of Articles 52 to 57 EPC as set out above makes it quite clear that even though agricultural methods in general are potentially patentable subject matter, the particular methods defined in Article 52(4) EPC are excluded from patentability. In other words, for the particular methods defined in Article 52(4) EPC, Article 52(4) EPC takes precedence over Article 57 EPC.[15]

Thus, a claimed method which by its terms is susceptible of industrial application, but which by its terms also falls within the wording of Article 52(4) EPC, must be regarded as not susceptible of industrial application and, therefore, excluded from patentability.

(c) Treatment by surgery

8–11   The term "surgery" is not limited to operations upon a human or animal body using invasive instruments, but includes also many other kinds of medical and veterinary procedures.

A claimed method ("for measuring bloodflow to a specific tissue of an animal") which includes a surgical step, but which also includes the step of sacrificing the animal, is not a method which is excluded from patentability under Article 52(4) EPC.[16]

---

[14] T116/85 O.J. EPO 1989, 13.
[15] Ibid.
[16] T182/90 O.J. EPO 1994, 641, July 30, 1993 (P).

(d) Treatment by therapy

(i) Introduction

Both prophylactic and curative treatments of disease are within the 8–12 meaning of the word "therapy" in Article 52(4) EPC, since both are directed to the same objective, *i.e.* the maintenance or restoration of health.[17]

There is no basis in law for distinguising between external and internal treatment: both constitute treatment by therapy.

Similarly, treatment of either a temporary or a permanent condition constitutes treatment by therapy.[18]

(ii) Cosmetic treatment compared with therapy

Several cases have dealt with situations where a particular compound 8–13 produces both cosmetic and medically beneficial effects, and where such effects overlap to a greater or lesser extent.

The situation is complicated by the fact that, if the compound *per se* is already known, then in the case of a non-medical (*e.g.* cosmetic) effect, the method of treatment or use may be claimed as such, but in the case of a medical effect, the further medical use may only be claimed in the form:

"use of a substance for the manufacture of a medicament for a specified therapeutic application" (see paragraph 10–30).

Whether or not a claimed invention is excluded from patentability under Article 52(4) EPC depends in particular upon the wording of the claim in question.[19]

Cosmetic compared with medical skin treatment: both effects claimed. In an appropriate case such as this, an application or patent may contain claims in appropriate from both to a medical and a non-medical (*e.g.* cosmetic) effect of a compound previously known *per se*.[20]

Appetite suppressant: cosmetic effect claimed. The fact that a chemical product has both a cosmetic and therapeutic effect when used to treat the human or animal body does not render the cosmetic treatment unpatentable, provided that according to the wording of the claim, protection is sought for the cosmetic treatment but not for the therapeutic treatment as such ("Method of improving the bodily appearance of a . . . mammal, which comprises orally administering [compound x] . . . in a dosage effective to reduce appetite, and repeating until a cosmetically beneficial loss of weight has occurred").[21]

Cleaning plaque from teeth: a further medical effect. However, in a case where the wording of the claims is directed to a technical effect ("A

---

[17] T19/86 O.J. EPO 1989, 24.
[18] T116/85 O.J. EPO 1989, 13.
[19] T290/86 O.J. EPO 1992, 414.
[20] T36/83 O.J. EPO 1986, 295.
[21] T144/83 O.J. EPO 1986, 301.

method of cleaning plaque and/or stains from human teeth . . .") which inevitably has a therapeutic effect as well as a cosmetic effect, such claims necessarily define a therapeutic treatment as well as a cosmetic treatment and are therefore excluded from patentability under Article 52(4) EPC.[22]

(ii) Non-therapeutic methods

8–14   A distinction is drawn between inventions involving treatment of the human or animal body for therapeutic purposes, and inventions involving physical activities carreed out on a human or animal body for purposes other than therapy: for example, a method of preventing piglets from suffocating under their dam, by sensing when the dam stands up, and creating conditions under her to discourage piglets from that area,[23] or the measurement and control of the flow of a drug-containing liquid passing through a device implanted in a human body.[24] Such methods are not excluded from patentability.

(e) Diagnostic methods

8–15   This exclusion has been narrowly construed. A diagnostic method is practised on the human body only if both examination and establishing the symptoms on the basis of the examination results are performed on a living human or animal body. Furthermore, the only diagnostic methods to be excluded from patent protection are those whose results immediately make it possible to decide on a particular course of medical treatment. Methods providing only interim results are thus not excluded, even if they can be utilised in making a diagnosis.[25]

D. Inventions Contrary to "Ordre Public" or Morality: Exceptions Under Article 53(a) EPC

8–16   Inventions the publication or exploitation of which would be contrary to "ordre public" or morality are not patentable. So far this exception to patentability has rarely been considered in actual cases, and its scope is therefore uncertain. In one important case,[26] which concerned the genetic manipulation of animals, it was held that it was necessary to consider Article 53(a) in relation to the issue of patentability, and that the decision as to whether or not Article 53(a) EPC is a bar to patenting such an invention would seem to depend mainly on a careful weighing up of the suffering of animals and possible risks to the environment on the one hand, and the invention's usefulness to mankind on the other.

The case was remitted to the Examining Division for consideration of this issue, and subsequently the patent was granted, but at the time of writing, the patent is under opposition.

---

[22] T290/86 O.J. EPO 1992, 414.
[23] T58/87 [1989] EPOR 125.
[24] T245/87 O.J. EPO 1989, 171.
[25] T384/86 O.J. EPO 1988, 308.
[26] T19/90 O.J. EPO 1990, 476.

This exception to patentability is potentially applicable to all European applications and patents, but is currently of particlar importance in the field of biotechnology.

E. PLANT AND ANIMAL VARIETIES, AND ESSENTIALLY BIOLOGICAL PROCESSES: EXCEPTIONS UNDER ARTICLE 53(B) EPC

(a) The nature of these exceptions

These exceptions can be classified as follows: 8–17

(a) Plant and animal varieties, *i.e.*:
  (i) plant varieties;
  (ii) animal varieties.
(b) Essentially biological processes for the production of plants and animals, *i.e.*
  (i) such processes for the production of plants;
  (ii) such processes for the production of animals;

This provision is not applicable to microbiological processes or the products thereof.

The relatively recent growth of biotechnology has made determination of the scope of the provisions in Article 53(b) EPC also increasingly critical.

It can be seen that no distinction is drawn between plants and animals, both forms of living matter being treated equally.

Before the EPC came into force, under earlier European national patent laws, living matter was generally excluded from patentability. The underlying reason for this was an ethical objection to intellectual property protection for any form of life. It has been possible to obtain legal protection for plant varieties since 1961, however.

(b) Plant varieties

(i) Background

The international Convention for the protection of New Varieties of 8–18 Plants, (known as the "UPOV Convention") was signed in 1961.

The UPOV Convention recognises monopoly rights for new plant varieties, as provided under appropriate national laws. Furthermore, under Article 2(1) of the UPOV Convention, the Member States agreed in principle to prohibit "double protection" in respect of the rights recognised by the Convention: either a special "plant breeders right" may be granted, or patent protection, but not both, in respect of plant varieties to which the Convention applies. While the exact extent of this prohibition and its application in individual countries is a matter for specific consideration and is not relevant here, nevertheless, its existence is indirectly relevant to the interpretation of Article 53(b) EPC. In particular, it has been recognised (see below) that Article 53(b) EPC is intended to express a general intention to exclude patent protection for subject matter capable of protection within the UPOV Convention.[27]

(ii) The meaning of "plant varieties"

The term "plant varieties" means a multiplicity of plants which are leagely the same in their characteristics and remain the same within specific tolerances after every propagation or every propagation cycle. This definition is reflected in the UPOV Convention, which is intended to give the breeder of a new plant variety a legal protective right. Plant varieties in this sense are all cultivated varieties, clones, lines, strains and hybrids which can be grown in such a way that they are clearly distinguishable from other varieties, which are sufficiently homogenous, and which are stable in their essential characteristics. Patent protection under the EPC was not intended for plant varieties of this kind, whether in the form of propagating material or of the plant itself.[28]

Thus, plant varieties are to be distinguished from plants, only the former being excluded from patentability under Article 53(b) EPC.

(c) Animal varieties

(i) Background

8–19   In contrast to plant varieties, which as discussed above may receive legal protection as a result of the UPOV Convention, no alternative form of legal protection is available for animal varieties.

The possibility of patent protection in respect of any form of animal life is a relatively new concept, as discussed above, and is a controversial matter. The extent to which animal life is patentable under the EPC will have to be decided through individual cases, primarily as a matter of interpretation of the provisions of sub-paragraphs (a) and (b) of Article 53 EPC, and the inter-relationship of these sub-paragraphs.

(ii) The distinction between animal varieties and animals

There has been so far only one case[29] dealing with this distinction. The claimed invention concerned in particular a transgenic mouse having cells "containing an activated oncogene sequence" introduced into it.

The Examining Division originally refused the application, but the Board of Appeal held that the exception to patentability under Article 53(b) EPC applies to certain categories of animals but not to animals as such.

Since the Examining Division had not considered the application on that basis, the case was remitted for further examination as to whether or not the subject matter of the application was an "animal variety". The

---

[27] T49/83 O.J. EPO 1984, 112.
[28] T49/83 O.J. EPO 1984, 112; T320/87 O.J. EPO 1990, 71.
[29] T19/90 O.J. EPO 1990, 476.

Examining Division subsequently granted the patent, and at the time of writing the patent is under opposition.

(d) Essentially biological processes for the production of plants and animals

(i) The distinction between biology and micro-biology

The importance of this distinction derives from the final part of Article 53(b) EPC, which provides that the previously defined exceptions to patentability "do not apply to microbiological processes or the products thereof". Thus, the EPC specifically makes it clear that, at least at the microbe level, living matter is in principle patentable. Consequently, European patents are commonly granted for micro-organisms *per se*, whether merely isolated from nature or when genetically changes, as well as for their components, *i.e.* specific DNA sequences, plasmids, etc.

8–20

(ii) The distinction between biological and non-biological processes

A particular process may clearly be not a microbiological process, but concerned with the production of plants or animals. The question may then arise as to whether the process falls within the exception of Article 53(b) EPC. This depends on the extent to which there is intervention by man in the process, and the process has to be judged on the basis of the essence of the invention taking into account the totality of human intervention and its impact on the result achieved.[30]

F. SUSCEPTIBLE OF INDUSTRIAL APPLICATION: ARTICLE 57 EPC

According to Article 57 EPC an invention shall be considered as susceptible of industrial application if it can be made or used in any kind of industry.

8–21

The requirement is satisfied if the claimed invention can be used by enterprises whose object is to beautify the human or animal body.

Such enterprises in the cosmetic field—such as cosmetic salons and beauty parlours—are considered to be a part of industry since this concept implies that an activity is carried out continuously, independently and for financial gain.[31]

A method involving interaction with the human or animal body is susceptible of industrial application if it can be used with the desired result by a technician without specialist medical knowledge and skills.[32]

---

[30] T320/87 O.J. EPO 1990, 71.
[31] T144/83 O.J. EPO 1986, 301; T36/83 O.J. EPO 1986, 295.
[32] T385/86 O.J. EPO 1988, 308.

9. Priority

CONTENTS

A. INTRODUCTION

(a) Outline of the priority system

9–01   An applicant for a European patent may claim priority for his application from the filing date of an earlier application in an individual country which is a party to the Paris Convention (a "Convention country") filed within the previous 12 months. The success or otherwise of such a claim to priority determines whether the claimed invention, the subject of the European application, is examined for novelty and inventive step at the filing date of the earlier application or at the filing date of the European application (Article 89 EPC). The principles which govern the claiming of priority are therefore discussed in this chapter, and the principles governing the determination of novelty and inventive step are then respectively considered in Chapters 10 and 11.

The system of priority rights under the EPC, and the effects of this system, are governed by Articles 87 to 89 EPC, which, together with Rule 38 EPC, form a complete, self-contained code of rules of law on the subject of claiming priority for the purpose of filing a European patent application. The language of some of these provisions is, to a large extent, taken from that used in Article 4 of the Paris Convention.[1] However, this code of rules of law is, and was designed to be, independent of the Paris Convention.[2]

(b) Relationship between the EPC and the Paris Convention

The preamble to the EPC states that the Contracting States were 9–02 "desiring . . . to conclude a Convention . . . which constitutes a special agreement within the meaning of Article 19 Paris . . .". Article 19 Paris provides that the Union countries may make special agreements between themselves for the protection of industrial property "insofar as these agreements do not contravene the provisions of this Convention."

Thus, the EPC constitutes a special agreement within the meaning of Article 19 Paris, whose relevant provisions are "clearly intended not to contravene the basic principles of priority laid down in the Paris Convention."[3]

(c) Background considerations

When considering priority, the following factors need to be born in 9–03 mind as general background:

(i) Having filed a first application in respect of an invention, an applicant has one year in which to decide in what other countries he wants to apply for patent protection. This decision is commonly related to commercial prospects, and in order to assess and promote such commercial prospects, the subject matter of his first application needs to be disclosed, without putting at risk the potential international patent protection in respect of the invention.

(ii) During the priority year following a first application the inventive subject matter commonly becomes improved and refined, and such improvements may or may not justify being made the subject of ancillary patent applications during the year. This situation is recognised by the possibility of multiple and partial priorities provided for both in the Paris Convention and in the EPC.

There may be cases, however, where such an improvement or refinement is within the general disclosure of the earlier application, but not fully worked out at that time. The question is then whether a claim which includes such improvement is still entitled to claim priority from the general disclosure in the earlier application.

(iii) It is also part of the normal course of events that an applicant has a much better idea of the proper scope of his claimed invention one year after the filing of the basic application, both in relation to the prior art and in relation to obtaining a fair protection for what has been invented.

---

[1] Convention for the Protection of Industrial Property, signed Paris 1883 amended Stockholm, 1967 ("the Paris Convention").
[2] J15/80 O.J. EPO 1981, 213; G2/93 O.J. EPO (P).
[3] T301/87 O.J. EPO 1990, 355; G2/93 O.J. EPO (P).

(iv) Regardless of scope, the actual working used in the claims to define the invention can also often be improved. Bearing in mind that the subject matter of a patent application commonly comprises creative thinking, it is not always immediately easy to describe and define such subject matter in the most appropriate way, especially when under pressure to file a patent application as soon as possible in order to establish the earliest possible priority date.

B. THE PRIORITY SYSTEM UNDER THE EPC

(a) Nature of the earlier application

9–04   Article 87(1) EPC provides a priority right during a period of 12 months for a person who has duly filed an application in a Convention country for one of the following species of industrial property:

(i) a patent;
(ii) a registration of a utility model;
(iii) a utility certificate;
(iv) an inventor's certificate.

A priority right based on the deposit of an industrial design is not recognised for a European patent application.[4]

(b) Entitlement to priority

(i) Introduction: disclosure of the same invention

9–05   An applicant for a European patent is only entitled to claim priority from an earlier filed application if the European application is "in respect of the same invention" (Article 87(1) EPC).

The basic question is normally whether there is a disclosure of all the claimed features of the invention in the priority document. In relation to the question of disclosure, the same principles have often been applied as are applied in relation to novelty: that is, is the subject matter of the claim directly and unambiguously derivable from the disclosure in the priority document?

However, a technical feature may be included in a claim which does not affect the essential character and nature of the invention as such, in which cases the omission of such a technical feature from the priority document may not affect the fact that the same invention is both disclosed in the priority document and defined in the claim for which priority is claimed. In such a case the claim to priority may then be upheld.[5]

In deciding priority, the important question is whether or not features which are related to the character and technical effect of the invention (*i.e.*

---

[4] J15/80 O.J. EPO 1981, 213.
[5] T73/88 O.J. EPO 1992, 557.

the essential features) have been disclosed in the priority document: this consideration is normally central to determining whether the claims are "in respect of the same invention" as the disclosure in the priority document.

(ii) Express or implied disclosure of essential features

The disclosure of the essential features of the claimed invention in the 9–06 earlier application must either be express, or be directly and unambiguously implied. Missing features which are recognised as essential to the invention only later on are thus not part of the disclosure.[6]

(iii) General disclosures

The normal rule is that a general disclosure in the priority document 9–07 does not establish priority for a later claim to an undisclosed specific example within such general disclosure. For example, a claim defining a specific chemical compound is not entitled to priority from an earlier application containing a genetic disclosure covering the specific compound.[7]

One case concerned whether priority could be claimed from a general disclosure in an earlier application which encompassed two possible alternatives, in respect of a claim which included only one of the two alternatives.[8] Priority was refused because the claimed alternative was a necessary functional limitation for the invention, which reflected the discovery that not all variants of general disclosure in the earlier application worked adequately, and the necessity of such functional limitation to the invention was not adequately disclosed in the earlier application.

If an entity itself is disclosed to the skilled person in an earlier application, this does not necessarily mean that a component part of that entity is also disclosed for the purpose of priority, if this is not envisaged directly and unambiguously as such, and requires considerable investigation to reveal its identity.[9]

(iv) Disclosure of a claim

When considering what is disclosed by a claim of a priority document it 9–08 is relevant that the purpose of the claim is to define the protection which is sought. The fact that a claim in a priority document is broad enough to cover specific subject matter claimed for the first time in a European patent application cannot by itself be sufficient evidence that such subject matter has already been disclosed in the priority document so as to establish identity of invention for the purpose of claiming priority under Article 87 EPC.[10]

---

[6] T81/87 O.J. EPO 1990, 250.
[7] T85/87 [1989] EPOR 24.
[8] T61/85 [1988] EPOR 20.
[9] T301/87 O.J. EPO 1990, 335.
[10] T409/90 O.J. EPO 1993, 40.

(v) Essential and inessential features for the purpose of priority

9–09 For priority purposes, when a particular feature in the claims of the European application is not specifically disclosed in the priority document, it has to be considered whether the presence of that feature changed the character and nature of the claimed invention as such in comparison with what is disclosed in the priority document. If not, there is no loss of priority.

Whether a particular claimed feature is essential for the purpose of priority, and therefore needs to be specifically disclosed in the priority document, depends upon its relationship to the function and effect of the invention, and therefore to the character and nature of the invention. The inclusion of a technical feature in a claim which is an essential feature for the purpose of determining the scope of protection conferred is not necessarily an essential feature for the purpose of determining priority.[11]

In particular, a feature which is added to a claim after the priority date and which does not constitute an essential element of the invention but which is simply a voluntary limitation to the scope of the claim does not invalidate the claim to priority.[12]

(vi) Enabling disclosure

9–10 A priority document should contain a disclosure which enables the claimed invention to be carried out by a skilled person if it is to support a claim to priority. If this were not so, it could become a misuse of the priority system if some parties in a competitive situation were allowed to jump ahead of others on the basis of mere expectation or speculation set out in the priority document, without sufficient disclosure as to how to perform the invention.[13]

(vii) Priority application not the first filing

9–11 Objection to the claiming of priority may be based upon the ground that the priority application was not the first filed application in respect of the invention, and that an earlier application in respect of the same invention had been filed more than 12 months before the European application, by the same applicant (or his predecessors in title).

The same principles as regards the question of identity of invention discussed above are also applied in such cases.[14] In particular, a patent application cannot serve as a basis for claiming a right of priority under Article 87(1) EPC where an application has been filed prior to the said application and this subsequent application is distinguished from the previous application only by a limitation of the scope of protection (e.g. a disclaimer) which does not change the nature of the invention.[15]

---

[11] T73/88 O.J. EPO 1992, 557.
[12] T16/87 O.J. EPO 1992, 212; T582/91 November 11, 1992.
[13] T81/87 O.J. EPO 1990, 250.
[14] T184/84 [1986] EPOR 169; T295/87 O.J. EPO 1990, 470.
[15] T255/91 O.J. EPO 1993, 318.

(viii) Intervening publication by the applicant of the contents of a priority document

When an applicant files an application in a Convention country (see 9–12 paragraph 9–01) in respect of an invention with subject matter A, and subsequently files a European application claiming priority from the earlier application and containing claims for example, both in respect of subject matter A and in respect of subject matter A and B relating to developments in the original subject matter A, the question arises whether disclosure to the public of subject matter A by the applicant during the priority period between the filing of the earlier application (the priority document) and the filing of the European application forms part of the state of the art on which an allegation of lack of inventive step in subject matter A and B may be based, in the case where the claims in respect of subject matter A and B are held not to be entitled to priority from the earlier application because they are not "in respect of the same invention" as the subject matter A in the earlier application.

Although in an earlier decision of a Board of Appeal it was held, on the basis of Article 4B of the Paris Convention, that an applicant is protected from the consequences of his own publication of the subject matter contained in the priority document during the priority period,[16] this decision was subsequently overruled by an Opinion of the Enlarged Board of Appeal. In this Opinion it was held that, under the EPC, the disclosure by the applicant of the subject matter contained in the priority document during the priority period does constitute prior art which is citable against a European application claiming priority from the priority document, to the extent that the claims of the European application are not entitled to the claimed priority.[17]

Thus, following the filing of an initial application for an invention in a Convention country, during the subsequent priority year prior to the filing of a European application, an applicant must take care not to disclose such invention, except in confidence. Any disclosure to the public of such invention may endanger the validity of claims which are included in a subsequent European application in respect of developments in the original subject matter (*e.g.* A and B), under the system of multiple priorities (see paragraph 9–03 above).

(ix) Successors in title

The right of priority belongs in the first place to the original applicant 9–13 (Article 87(1) EPC). Being a legal right, it is assignable in law, as is recognised by the reference to "successors in title."

The validity of an assignment of a priority right is a matter for the law in the country where the assignment is made. In proceedings before the EPO any relevant national law has to be established and proved by suitable evidence.[18]

---

[16] T301/87 O.J. EPO 1990, 335.
[17] G2/93 O.J. EPO(P).
[18] J19/87 March 21, 1988.

10. Novelty

CONTENTS

A. INTRODUCTION

(a) Preliminary considerations

Articles 54 and 56 EPC deal respectively with the requirements of **10–01** novelty and inventive step as prerequisites for patentability.

The first step in relation to both requirements is the determination of what constitutes the state of the art, as defined in Article 54(2) EPC. The second step in relation to the requirement of novelty is to determine whether the subject matter claimed in the European patent application or patent "forms part of the state of the art" (Article 54(1) EPC). The second step in relation to the requirement of inventive step is to determine whether the claimed subject matter was or was not "obvious to a person skilled in the art" (Article 56 EPC, first sentence, and see Chapter 11). The latter determination pre-supposes that the claimed subject matter is not part of the state of the art.

(b) The basic requirements for novelty

The essence of Article 54(1) EPC in conjunction with Article 52(1) EPC **10–02** is that what already forms part of the state of the art cannot be patented, because it is not new.

In relation to the question of novelty of a claimed invention, there are in principle two quite distinct matters to be considered:

(i) What is within the "state of the art"?
(ii) Is the claimed invention novel over the state of the art?

As to (i), the "state of the art" at the filing date of an application falls into two categories:

(1) Published prior art — *i.e.* that which has been "made available to the public", such as prior published documents, prior used products, etc. (Article 54(2) EPC).
(2) Prior rights — *i.e.* the content of European patent applications as filed, which have been filed but not published (Article 54(3) EPC).

These two categories of the state of the art are considered separately in section B below.

As to (ii), this question is considered in section C, "Substantive Novelty" below.

(c) The dual concept of "made available to the public"

In relation to the published prior art, it follows from the wording of **10–03** Article 54(2) EPC that the requirement of novelty involves two separate and sequential inquiries as to what was "made available to the public", namely:

(i) What has been made available to the public in the physical sense (by physical means such as a document, a prior used product, etc.).
(ii) What information in the form of a technical teaching has been made available to a skilled person, as a result of the physical means having been made available?

The first question is considered within section B, "The State of the Art," and the second question is considered within section C, "Substantive novelty," below.

B. THE STATE OF THE ART

(a) Published prior art: Article 54(2) EPC

(i) Introduction

10–04 **The concept of "made available to the public".** The published prior art in relation to an application includes all information that has been "made available to the public" at the filing date of the application. Information may become part of the published prior art by any means (by written or oral description, by use, or in any other way — see Article 54(2) EPC). Whatever the means of disclosure, availability in the sense of Article 52(2) EPC involves two separate stages: availability of the means of disclosure, and availability of information which is accessible and deriveable from such means.[1]

It is not necessary that any particular member of the public actually received information before the relevant filing date. What matters is whether such information was made available before that date.

Scale of availability. The scale on which information has been made available to the public is, in principle, irrelevant. Thus, a single copy of a document or a single sale of an apparatus[2] is sufficient.

Similary "the public" in this context comprises a single member of the public, or any greater number.

Where available. Information which is "made available to the public" anywhere in the world "forms part of the state of the art" and is therefore part of the published prior art for the purpose of Article 54 EPC.

When available. Information may become part of the published prior art for the purpose of Article 54 EPC at any point in time before the filing date.

Confidentiality. Information that has been made available to one or more third parties, in confidence, is secret and has not been made available "to the public". Whether particular information that has been made available to other persons was secret or confidential in the sense that it

---

[1] T952/92 O.J. EPO (P).
[2] T381/87 O.J. 1990, 213; T482/89 O.J. EPO 1992, 646.

was subject to restrictions as to its further disclosure or use is a question of fact to be decided according to the circumstances in each individual case.

If access to a document is deliberately restricted to certain persons it is not available to the public, even if the group of persons able to gain knowledge of the content of the document is large.[3]

Availability a question of fact. Whatever the physical means by which information is made available to the public (*e.g.* written description, oral description, use, pictorial description on a film or in a photograph, etc., or a combination of such means), the question of what has been made available to the public is one of fact in each case.[4]

Thus, in some cases, an initial question may arise as to whether a physical means such as a written description or a product was in fact "made available to the public".

(ii) Publication by written description

In this case, where the written description is in the form of a patent 10–05 specification or any other document, the content of the document is admissible prior art if the document was in a place to which members of the public had access. For example, a document which is proved to have been on the shelves of a public library is part of the published prior art, regardless of whether any person looked at it.

In almost all cases, the date of publication of a prior art document is not in dispute. Occasionally, however, the facts relating to publication may be seriously in dispute, and crucial to patentability.

Example. In one case,[5] an article written by the inventors in respect of a subsequent European patent application was contained in a journal.

1. Copies of the journal were sent to subscribers in the United Kingdom by second class post two days before the filing date of the patent application. On the evidence no subscriber received it before the filing date. It was held that the document was not "made available to the public" merely by being addressed to a member of the public and placed in a post-box. At all times prior to its delivery to the person to whom it was addressed, it was not "available to the public."

2. One copy of the journal was also sent by the publishers directly to a library, and arrived there the day before the filing date. On the evidence, the journal was placed on the shelves of the library on the same day.

It was held that the document formed part of the state of the art for the purpose of Article 54 EPC on that day.

(iii) Publication by "oral description"

The same principles are applicable to an oral description, such as a 10–06 lecture. In the absence of a record of an oral description, difficulties may often arise in determining what was made available to the public.

---

[3] T300/86 O.J. EPO August 28, 1989.
[4] G2/88 O.J. EPO 1990, 93.
[5] T381/87 O.J. EPO 1990, 213.

(iv) Publication by use

10–07   The same principles are also applicable to the determination of what forms part of the state of the art, having regard to an allegation of prior use.

In particular, if a product has been made available to the public before the filing date of an application, its composition or structure is part of the state of the art if the product could be analysed and reproduced by a skilled person, whether or not particular reasons can be identified for analysing it. Information as to the composition or internal structure of a prior sold product is made available to the public if direct and unambiguous access to such information is possible by means of known analytical techniques which were available for use by a skilled person before the filing date. The amount of work and time involved in carrying out such an analysis is in principle irrelevant to the determination of what was made available to the public.[6]

In a simple case, a product which has been used in public may, in the course of such use, visually communicate the features of its manufacture, and thus make such features "available to the public".[7] A single sale of a product is sufficient to make that product available to the public.[8] What is made available to the public as a result of prior use is a question of fact in each case.

(b) Exclusions from the published prior art: Article 55 EPC

(i) Non-prejudicial disclosures

10–08   Article 55 EPC set out two circumstances in which a disclosure that has become part of the published prior art is nevertheless excluded from consideration "for the application of Article 54 EPC."

These two circumstances are when, during the six months immediately preceding the filing of a European patent application, a disclosure of the invention takes place due to, or in consequence of:

(a) an evident abuse in relation to the applicant or his legal predecessor;
(b) a display of the invention at an official international exhibition.

(ii) Time period for non-prejudicial disclosures

10–09   Such a disclosure "shall not be taken into consideration if it occured no earlier than six months preceding 'the filing' of an application." There is ambiguity as to whether "the filing" of an application always refers to its actual filing date,[9] or whether it may refer to its priority date.[10] The former view is consistent with Article 89 EPC, which states that the priority date

---

[6] G1/92 O.J. EPO 1993, 277; T952/92 O.J. EPO (P).
[7] *e.g.* T84/83 [1979–85] EPOR: C: 796.
[8] T482/89 O.J. EPO 1992, 646.
[9] As stated *obiter* in T173/83 O.J. EPO 1987, 465.
[10] As held in an Opposition Division Decision (Passoni) [1992] EPOR 79.

counts as the filing date for the purposes of Articles 54(2) and (3) and 60(2) EPC, there being no reference to Article 55 EPC. However, there appears to be no logical reason why the "filing" of an application for the purpose of Article 55 EPC should be a different date from the "filing date" in Article 54 EPC.

(iii) "Evident abuse"

Disclosure due to, or in consequence of an evident abuse in relation to **10–10** the application or his legal predecessor is excluded from the published prior art under Article 55(1)(a) EPC.

The expression "an evident abuse" seems intended to cover cases such as when an inventor discloses an invention in confidence, but the invention is subsequently made available to the public in breach of confidence. For example, there would be evident abuse when a third party communicates information received from the applicant, without authorisation, and knowing that he is not permitted to do so, thus risking causing harm to the applicant.[11]

(iv) Display at an official international exhibition

Disclosure due to, or in consequence of such a display is excluded under **10–11** Article 55 EPC.

The display of the invention must be:

(a) by the applicant or his legal predecessor; and
(b) at an official or officially recognised international exhibition; the exhibition must fall within the terms of the Paris Convention on International Exhibitions, 1928 (as amended, Paris, 1972). A list of international exhibitions which have been registered under the Paris Convention is published in the Official Journal from time to time.[12] Furthermore:
(c) when filing the patent application, the applicant must state that the invention has been so displayed; and
(d) within four months of the filing date, the applicant must file a supporting certificate in accordance with Rule 23 EPC, together with an identification of the invention, authenticated by the authority at the exhibition which issued the certificate.

(c) Prior rights: Article 54(3) EPC

(i) Introduction

A first European patent application which has a filing date earlier than **10–12** the filing date of a second European application, but which has been published after the filing date of the second European application, is not a

---

[11] T173/83 O.J. EPO 1987, 465.
[12] See, e.g. O.J. EPO 1989, 156.

part of the published prior art under Article 54(2) EPC in respect of the second application; but the content of the first application as filed (the "whole contents") is comprised in the state of the art by reason of a legal fiction set out in Article 54(3) EPC, and may also, therefore, form the basis for an objection to grant or maintenance of a European patent on the ground of lack of novelty (Article 54(1) EPC).

The contents of applications which become part of "the state of the art" by virtue of Article 54(3) EPC are expressly excluded from consideration in deciding whether there has been an inventive step (Article 56, second sentence).

A basic principle underlying Article 54(3) EPC is to avoid (as far as possible) the granting of more than one European patent in respect of exactly the same invention. Article 54(4) EPC limits the application of Article 54(3) EPC to situations where the same Contracting States are designated in both first and second European patent applications. For any particular designated Contracting State, Article 54(3) EPC thereby prevents the grant of a patent in respect of an invention which has been described in another European patent application that has not been published but which has an earlier filing date, and designates the same Contracting State(s). The "collision" of European patents is thus generally avoided.

However, insofar as Article 54(3) EPC refers to European patent applications of earlier filing date, there is nothing in the EPC to prevent the grant of two or more European patent applications, designating the same Contracting States, and having exactly the same subject matter, in the unlikely but possible event that they have the same filing date.

(ii) National prior rights not within Article 54(3) EPC

10–13 It is only prior filed European patent applications that form part of the state of the art under Article 54(3) EPC. A prior national patent application (*i.e.* a "national prior right") is not a European patent application within the meaning of Article 54(3) EPC, and is accordingly not within the state of the art, for the purpose of Article 54(1) EPC.[13]

The prior right effect of national patent applications and patents upon European patent applications and patents and vice-versa is a matter for individual national laws, and is governed by Article 139(1) and (2) EPC. In each such case, the national law as to prior right effects is applicable.

What happens when there is "collision" between a European patent application or patent and a national patent application or patent having the same filing date, is similarly left to the individual national laws of the Contracting States, under Article 139(3) EPC.

An applicant may on his own initiative during examination proceedings submit different claims for those designated Contracting States in which pertinent prior national rights exist, so as to take account of the applicable national laws. Amended claims may also be proposed for the same reason

---

[13] T550/88 O.J. EPO 1992, 117.

during opposition proceedings, regardless of the grounds of opposition relied upon by the opponent.[14]

(iii) Avoidance of "self-collision"

The fact that the contents of prior filed patent applications are only **10–14** considered from the point of view of novelty, and not as regards inventive step, makes the distinction between novelty and inventive step an important one.

The exclusion of inventive step from consideration in relation to prior filed applications avoids the possibility of "self-collision."

Thus, having filed a first European application, an applicant may subsequently file one or more subsequent European applications in respect of developments to the subject matter of the first application, before publication of the basic application. Provided that the claimed subject matter of each such later application is novel over the contents of each of the earlier applications, such claimed subject matter is separately patentable.

C. Substantive Novelty

(a) Introduction

Substantive novelty is concerned with whether the claimed invention is **10–15** novel over the state of the art. A claim must define an invention in terms of its technical features (Rule 29(1) EPC). A claimed invention lacks novelty unless it includes at least one essential technical feature which distinguishes it from the state of the art.[15] Determination of novelty thus involves a comparison between the information, or technical teaching, which is within the state of the art, and the claimed invention. Such a comparison has to be made whatever the physical means by which the information is made available to the public. The majority of cases are concerned with the assessment of information which has been made available in published documents.

When deciding upon the novelty of a claim, a basic initial consideration is to construe the claim in order to determine its technical features. After that has been done, the further question to be considered is whether what has been "made available to the public" includes all of the claimed technical features.

The word "available" carries with it the idea that, for lack of novelty to be found, all the technical features of the claimed invention in combination must have been communicated to the public, or laid open for inspection.[16]

---

[14] See Rules 57a and 87 (in force from June 1, 1995).
[15] G2/88 O.J. EPO 1990, 93.
[16] Ibid.

The novelty of a claimed invention is destroyed by the prior disclosure (by any means) of an embodiment which falls within the claim.

(b) Importance of the distinction between lack of novelty and lack of inventive step

10–16   In many cases, it is not essential to draw a line between novelty and obviousness. If, for example, a prior document discloses the subject matter of a claimed invention except that there is some doubt as to identity of disclosure in respect of one feature of the claim, such a case may frequently be decided on the basis that even if that one feature is not actually disclosed in the prior document, the claimed subject matter including that one feature is nevertheless lacking an inventive step having regard to the teaching of the prior document.

There are, however, certain circumstances when the distinction between novelty and inventive step is particularly important. Two examples are:

(i) Under Article 54(3) EPC

When the prior art to be considered is not published prior art, but a prior filed European application (*i.e.* a prior right), then as stated in paragraph 10–12 above the only applicable ground of objection is lack of novelty, having regard to the content of that application. In this context, therefore, the distinction between lack of novelty and lack of inventive step can be crucial to the granting or maintenance of a European patent.[17]

(ii) "Accidental anticipation"

In a case where a prior document in the published prior art is not concerned with the same technical field as the claimed subject matter, but nevertheless "accidentally" discloses (or comes close to disclosing) all the features claimed, the determination of novelty may also be of crucial importance. A particular prior document may in such circumstances be considered as the closest prior art from the point of view of novelty determination, but not in relation to the question of inventive step.

(c) General principles

10–17   The purpose of Article 54(1) EPC is to prevent what is part of the state of the art from being patented.[18]

Since novelty is an absolute concept, a definition of an invention which differs only in wording is insufficient; what has to be established in the examination as to novelty is whether the state of the art is such as to make available the subject matter of the invention to the skilled person in a technical teaching.[19]

---

[17] See, *e.g.* T167/84 O.J. EPO 1987, 369.
[18] T12/81 O.J. EPO 1982, 296; T124/87 O.J. EPO 1989, 491.
[19] T198/84 O.J. EPO 1985, 209; T124/87 O.J. EPO 1989, 491.

When part of the state of the art is a written document, what has to be considered is whether the disclosure of the document as a whole is such as to make available to be a skilled person as a technical teaching the subject matter for which protection is sought in the claims of the disputed patent.[20] The question is whether the claimed invention could be derived directly and unmistakably from the prior document by a skilled person.[21]

(d) Consideration of individual documents in isolation

When assessing novelty, the disclosure of a particular prior document 10–18 must always be considered in isolation; in other words, it is only the actual content of a document (as undestood by a skilled person) which destroys novelty. It is not permissible to combine separate items of prior art together.[22] This is the general rule.

(e) Consideration of a document in its entirety

The technical teaching in a prior art document should be considered in 10–19 its entirety, as it would be done by a person skilled in the art. It is not justified arbitrarily to isolate parts of such document from their context in order to derive therefrom a technical information which would be distinct from or even in contradiction to the integral teaching of the document.[23]

(f) Incorporation of another document by reference

As an exception to the above general rule, in a case where there is a 10–20 specific reference in one prior document (the "primary document") to a second prior document, the presence of such specific reference may necessitate that part or all of the disclosure of the second document be considered as part of the disclosure of the primary document.[24] This depends upon the relevant wording and circumstances of each particular case.

(g) Erroneous disclosures

(i) Internal inconsistency within a prior document

If part of a prior document would be considered by a skilled reader to 10–21 be erroneous in its contest in the remainder of the document and would be corrected by such a reader, such document should not be read literally so as to deprive an application of novelty, but should be read as so corrected.[25]

---

[20] Ibid.
[21] T204/83 O.J. EPO 1985, 310; T56/87 O.J. EPO 1990, 188.
[22] T153/85 O.J. EPO 1988, 1; T77/87 O.J. EPO 1990, 280.
[23] T56/87 O.J. EPO 1990, 188.
[24] T153/85 O.J. EPO 1988, 1.
[25] T89/87 December 20, 1989.

(ii) Error in an abstract

In one case, an original document had been prior published as well as an abstract of it. In the abstract a particular ratio had been transposed as compared to the original document. With such transposition of the ratio, the abstract included a ratio which literally deprived a claim of novelty, whereas the corresponding ratio as stated in the original document did not cause loss of novelty. There was nothing inherently implausible in the literal contents of the abstract. Nevertheless, it was held that because the title of the abstract included a cross-reference to the original document, the disclosure of the abstract should be interpreted by reference to the original document, for the purpose of ascertaining the technical reality of what had been disclosed. Furthermore, the original document was considered as the primary source of technical teaching, the abstract by its nature being a secondary source. In such circumstances the disclosure of the original document was held to prevail with the result that the claimed invention was held to be novel.

Thus, when it is clear from related contemporaneously available evidence that the literal disclosure of a document is erroneous and does not represent the intended technical reality, such an erroneous disclosure should not be considered as part of the state of the art.[26]

(h) Novelty of well-known equivalents

10–22   It is not correct to interpret the teaching of a document as embracing well-known equivalents which are not disclosed in the document: this is a matter for obviousness.[27]

(i) Novelty as a matter of substance

10–23   Novelty must be substantive and not simply a matter of language. Furthermore, the concept of novelty must not be given such a narrow interpretation that only what has already been described in the same terms is prejudicial to it.[28] What is 'made available to the public' by specific detailed examples included in a document is not necessarily limited to the exact details of such specific examples but depends in each case upon the technical teaching which is made available to a skilled reader.[29]

(j) Inevitable result

10–24   In some circumstances, the inevitable result of what is described in a document may cause loss of novelty.[30] If carrying out what is specifically described in the prior art leads to a product which is the subject matter of

---

[26] 77/87 O.J. EPO 1990, 280.
[27] T167/84 O.J. EPO 1987, 369.
[28] T12/81 O.J. EPO 1982, 296.
[29] T290/86 O.J. EPO 1992, 414.
[30] G2/88 O.J. EPO 1990, 93; T12/81 O.J. EPO 1982, 296.

a claim, the claimed invention may lack novelty even though such product is not specifically described in the prior art.

A distinction should be made between a combination of starting material and process and combinations of two starting materials. A disclosure of the starting substance as well as the reaction process is always prejudicial to novelty because this combination unalterably establishes the end product. On the other hand, if two classes of starting materials are required to prepare the end product and examples of individual entities in each class are given in two lists of some length, then a substance resulting from the reaction of a specific pair from the two lists can nevertheless be regarded as new.[31]

(k) Disclosure in drawings

Features shown solely in a drawing form part of the state of the art 10–25 when a person skilled in that art is able, in the absence of any other description, to derive a technical teaching from them.[32] This is a question of fact in each case.

(l) Enabling disclosures

A chemical compound which has been defined in a prior document by 10–26 means of its chemical structure is only part of the state of the art if a skilled person is thereby able to obtain it. For example, a document does not effectively disclose a chemical compound, even though it states the structure and the steps by which it is produced, if the skilled person is unable to find out from the document or from common general knowledge how to obtain the required starting materials or intermediates.[33]

To destroy novelty, a document cited under Article 54(2) and (3) EPC must disclose the invention in a manner sufficiently clear and complete for it to be carried out by a man skilled in the art.[34]

(m) Overlapping ranges

In general terms, the technical teaching which is derivable by a skilled 10–27 person from a general disclosure such as a range of values for a parameter must depend upon a careful examination in each particular case of what is really taught in the prior document.

For example, if the preferred numerical range in a citation in part overlaps with a range claimed in an application, the said claimed range cannot be regarded as novel, at least in cases where the values in the examples given in the citation lie just outside the claimed range and teach the skilled person that it is possible to use the whole of this range.[35]

---

[31] *Ibid.*
[32] T204/83 O.J. EPO 1985, 310.
[33] T206/83 O.J. EPO 1987, 5.
[34] T81/87 O.J. EPO 1990, 250.
[35] T17/85 O.J. EPO 1986, 406.

In assessing the novelty of the invention compared to the prior art in a case where overlapping ranges of a certain parameter exist, it has to be considered whether the person skilled in the art would, in the light of the technical facts, seriously contemplate applying the technical teaching of the prior art document in the range of overlap. If it can be fairly assumed that he would do so it must be concluded that no novelty exists. However, if there exists in a prior art document disclosing a range of a parameter a reasoned statement dissuading the person skilled in the art from practising the technical teaching of the document in a certain part of the range, such part has to be regarded as novel for the purposes of Article 54 EPC.[36]

(n) Generic disclosures: selection inventions

10–28   In a number of cases (particularly chemical cases) the subject matter of a claim (*e.g.* a particular compound) is embraced by a general disclosure covering a larger area than the specific claimed subject matter (*e.g.* a class of compounds of which the particular compound is a member). In such situations, when determining novelty, a distinction should be drawn between an extensive general disclosure and a narrow sub-disclosure within it which has not been individualised.

In general terms, a generic disclosure does not usually take away the novelty of any specific example falling within the terms of that disclosure, but a specific disclosure does take away the novelty of a generic claim embracing that disclosure.

This approach to the assessment of novelty allows for the possibility of so-called "selection inventions", where inventiveness lies in a particular selection from a known field.

For example, in one case a prior document disclosed a catalytic process, and the claimed invention was the same catalytic process but required the use of an amount of catalyst within a specified range of percentages. It was held that since this sub-range was "narrow and sufficiently far removed from the known range illustrated by means of examples", the sub-range was "a quantitative range which had not yet been individualised" and was, therefore, new. It was further held that the use of the claimed amount of catalyst was inventive, having regard to the increased yield obtained only within the selected sub-range.[37]

In another case, a prior document disclosed di-substituted xanthines where the substituents had to be chosen from two different lists, and it had to be determined whether claims to a particular di-substituted xanthine with a particular combination of substituents were novel. It was held that a class of chemical compounds, defined only by a general structural formula having at least two variable groups does not specifically disclose each of the individual compounds which would result from the combination of all possible variants within such groups.[38]

---

[36] T26/85 O.J. EPO 1990, 22.
[37] T198/84 O.J. EPO 1985, 209.
[38] T9/86 O.J. EPO 1988, 381.

(o) Product-by-process claims

(i) A new process for making a known product

Such an invention is properly protected by a process claim in which the 10–29 result of carrying out the process steps is the production of the known product.

Article 64(2) EPC provides that "If the subject matter of the European patent is a process, the protection conferred by the patent shall extend to the products directly obtained by such process."

Having regard to such automatic product protection provided by a process claim, claims for products defined in terms of processes for their preparation (known as "product-by-process" claims) are admissible only if the products themselves fulfil the requirements for patentability.[39] Article 64(2) EPC does not confer novelty upon a claim which is formulated as a "product-by-process" when no novelty exists in such product *per se*, and does not entitle or enable an applicant for a European patent to include such claims in his patent which do not satisfy the requirements for patentability of Article 52(1) EPC.[40]

In other words, novelty is not conferred upon a product merely by reason of the history of its origin. If the product of a new process is in all respects identical with the product of a known process, there is no novelty either in a claim to the product *per se* of the new process, or in a claim to the product-by-(new) process.

(ii) A known process for making a new product: analogy process

Such an invention may be protected by a claim which defines the (known) process steps, the final step being the production of the new product.[41]

(p) Further uses of a known product

(i) Products for medical use

First medical use of a known product. Methods of treatment of the 10–30 human or animal body are excluded from patentability under Article 52(4) EPC (see paragraph 8–09). Article 54(5) EPC provides that a substance or composition for use in such a medical or veterinary method does not lack novelty, even when the substance or composition is itself part of the state of the art, provided that its use for any such medical or veterinary method is not comprised in the state of the art.

Second and further medical uses of a product having a known medical use. Prima facie, the wording of Article 54(5) EPC could be interpreted as meaning that if a product has already been used or disclosed for use in

---

[39] T150/82 O.J. EPO 1984, 309.
[40] T248/85 O.J. EPO 1986, 261.
[41] T119/82 O.J. EPO 1984, 217.

any pharmaceutical method so that a pharmaceutical use of the product is already part of the state of the art, a claim to a second or further pharmaceutical use of the product would lack novelty.

However, the question of the patentability of a second or further medical use was considered by the Enlarged Board of Appeal, and it was held that:

(a) claims directed to the use of a product for the treatment of an illness in a human or animal body (when such use was the second or subsequent medical use) were equivalent to claims for a method of treatment of the human or animal body, and therefore excluded from patentability by Article 52(4) EPC;

(b) claims directed to "the use of a substance for the manufacture of a medicament for a specified new therapeutic use" were not lacking in novelty for the purpose of Article 54 EPC.[42]

In reaching this conclusion as to the potential novelty and patentability of second and further medical uses, the Enlarged Board considered that it was justifiable, by analogy with the derivation of novelty for a first medical use from its new purpose in accordance with Article 54(5) EPC itself, to derive the novelty for such a use claim from the new therapeutic use of the medicament, irrespective of the fact of whether any pharmaceutic use of the medicament was already known or not.

In other words, because Article 54(5) EPC says that a first medical use is novel, implicitly because of the presence in the claim of the newly discovered medical use, the Enlarged Board held that second or further medical uses (claimed as set out above) were also novel on the same basis.

The justification for this extension of patent protection to second and subsequent medical uses clearly lies fundamentally in a reluctance to draw the line for patentability at the first medical use, there being no reason in equity or logic for so doing.

The nature of novelty in medical uses of a known product. In contrast to "normal" product claims where a prerequisite for novelty is that the product is defined in the claim has at least one physical parameter which distinguishes it from previously known products, in the case of a claim to "a product for use in a first or subsequent medical use" (whatever the exact form of the claim), the product *per se* as defined in the claim does not need to be physically distinguishable from previously known products, for the claim to be novel.

(ii) Further non-medical use of a known product

10–31 **Introduction.** In connection with non-medical inventions, there is obviously no potential difficulty in claiming new methods of using a known product where the methods steps themselves are new, *i.e.* where there is a novelty in the physical activity by the claim.

---

[42] G5/83 O.J. EPO 1985, 64.

Difficulty arises as far as the question of novelty is concerned, however, when there is no novelty in the physical activity required for the carrying out of a new use of a known product, *i.e.* when a known product is used to achieve a new purpose or effect. In this case, no "special concept" of novelty can be derived from the EPC (*cf.* Article 54(5) EPC, discussed in paragraph 10–30 above).

On the other hand (as with medical inventions concerning further medical uses of a known product), when a product is known to have a particular use, there is, in principle, a proper basis for a patentable invention in the discovery of a further non-obvious use of the same product. Whether the carrying out of such a further use requires the same or a different physical activity is essentially an artificial distinction.

Interpretation of use claims. In relation to a use claim defining a new use (*i.e.* purpose) for a known compound, having regard to Article 69 EPC and its Protocol where a particular technical effect which underlies such use is described in the patent, the proper interpretatioin of the claim will require that a functional feature should be implied into the claim, as a technical feature; for example, that the compound actually achieves the particular described effect.[43]

The novelty question: "inherent" compared with "made available". If, on its interpretation in accordance with Article 69 EPC, a claim to a further use of a known entity includes such a functional technical feature, the novelty of the claim may depend upon whether this functional technical feature (in combination with the other claimed features) has been "made available to the public."

Under Article 54(2) EPC the question to be decided is what has been made available to the public: the question is not what may have been "inherent" in what was made available (by a prior written description, or by what has previously been used, for example). Under the EPC, a hidden or secret use, because it had not been made available to the public, is not a ground of objection to validity of a European patent.

The fact that a particular product has been used, or disclosed for use, for a particular previously known purpose based upon a known technical effect of that product, does not destroy the novelty in a claim which (on its proper interpretation in accordance with Article 69 EPC) includes a functional feature defining a new use for a new purpose in accordance with a technical effect which was inherently achieved during the prior use for the previously known purpose, provided that such technical effect underlying the new use remained hidden during such prior use and was, therefore, not made available to the public.[44] Whether a previously undisclosed technical effect, which in fact inevitably occurs when a previously disclosed technical teaching is carried out, has thereby been made available to the public is a question of fact which has to be decided in the context of each individual case.[45]

---

[43] G2/88 O.J. EPO 1990, 93.
[44] *Ibid.*
[45] T59/87 O.J. EPO 1991, 561.

The nature of novelty in a new non-medical use of a known product. As with first and subsequent medical use claims, the product *per se*, which is defined in the claim, does not need to be physically distinguishable from previously known products in order for the claim to be novel.

However, in contrast to first and subsequent medical use claims, the novelty in a "new non-medical use" claim is not derived either directly or analogously from the provision of Article 54(5) EPC, but is derived from the general principle that a claim is novel if it includes at least one technical feature that distinguishes it from the state of the art because such technical feature has not been "made available to the public."

11. Inventive Step

CONTENTS

A. INTRODUCTION

(a) Principles of assessment

11–01   Determination of the question whether a claimed invention involves an inventive step takes place if it has been established that the combination of claimed technical features is not part of the state of the art, and that the claimed invention is therefore novel.

Article 56 EPC states that "An invention shall be considered as involving an inventive step if, having regard to the state of the art, it is not obvious to a person skilled in the art."

Since the "state of the art" is defined in Article 54(2) EPC as comprising "everything made available to the public . . . before the date of filing of the European patent application," the date at which the state of the art has to be assessed for inventive step is the filing date. The filing date of an application is either the actual filing date, or if the application is entitled to a right of priority under Article 87 EPC (see Chapter 9), then the date of priority counts as the filing date by virtue of Article 89 EPC.

As to what constitutes the "state of the art", or "published prior art", see paragraphs 10–04 *et seq.*

The majority of appeals which are decided by the Technical Boards of Appeal are concerned with the assessment of inventive step, and are decided upon their individual facts. Nevertheless, a number of decisions of the Boards of Appeal have emphasised points of legal principle which underlie the assessment of inventive step in accordance with the EPC, and which should be taken into account in particular cases.

The most important and distinctive principle which is generally applied within the EPO is referred to as the "problem-and-solution" approach to the assessment of inventive step, and this is considered below.

(b) Standard of inventiveness

11–02   Patents granted under the EPC should have inventive step sufficient to ensure to the patentees a fair degree of certainty that if contested the validity of the patent will be upheld by a national court. The standard should not be below what may be considered an average amongst the standards presently applied by the Contracting States.[1]

B. THE PROBLEM-AND-SOLUTION APPROACH

(a) Basic principles

11–03   The basic sequence of the problem-and-solution approach may be summarised as follows:

(i) With reference to the claimed invention to be assessed, the "closest prior art" is determined (for example, the prior document which comes closest to disclosing the invention).

---

[1] T1/81 O.J. EPO 1981, 439.

(ii) Starting from this closest prior art and the technical results or effect achieved thereby, and by comparison with the technical effect achieved by the claimed invention, the objective technical problem to be solved in progressing from the closest prior art to the claimed invention is determined.

(iii) The obviousness or otherwise of the proposed solution to this problem to a person skilled in the art starting from the closest prior art is assessed.

(b) Characteristics

Particular characteristics of this problem-and-solution approach are as follows: **11–04**

(i) The assessment of inventive step is essentially objective.

(ii) The presence or absence of an inventive step is predominantly determined on the basis of a technical assessment of the inventiveness of the advance made from the closest prior art to the claimed invention.

(iii) Having assessed inventive step starting from the closest prior art, there should be no need for further consideration of inventiveness starting from other less relevant prior art.

An advantage of the regular use of the problem-and-solution approach for the assessment of inventive step in proceedings before the EPO, as opposed to a more random consideration of various potentially relevant factors indicating the presence of absence of inventive step which may arise on a case-to-case basis, is that a consistent standard of inventiveness as a criterion for the grant or maintenance of European patents should be maintained.

The adoption of a consistent standard of inventiveness for European patents has been regarded as highly imnportant during the initial years of operation of the EPO, in order that public confidence in the inventive merit underlying the subject matter of such patents should be sustained. For this reason the use of the problem-and-solution approach has been strongly advocated in a number of Board of Appeal decisions, and is official policy during first instance procedure.

C. Identification of the Closest prior Art

(a) General considerations

An objective assessment of inventive step starting from the closest prior **11–05** art implies that the latter has been positively identified and considered.[2]

The closest prior art is that which forms the best starting point within the state of the art from which the claimed invention could have been

---

[2] T248/85 O.J. EPO 1986, 261.

made, *i.e.* the most promising springboard towards the invention which was available to the skilled person at the filing date.[3] Frequently, the prior art which has the most technical features in common with the claimed invention and which is in the same technical field of application will be the closest prior art. In many cases, however, the prior art which is the most closely concerned with the problem underlying the claimed invention will be considered as the closest prior art.

In a few cases there is controversy as to what should be considered to constitute the closest prior art document, and it may then be sensible to assess inventive step starting from more than one document in the alternative.

(b) Patent publications compared with commercial state of the art

11–06   Commercial publications and products are to be assessed at the same level as patent and other technical literature when identifying the closest prior art, even though the former may represent current actual practice. In assessing inventive step the person skilled in the art when looking for a solution to a problem is presumed to study patent publications in the relevant patent classes with particular interest.[4] This is in accordance with commercial practice, since patent specifications are recognized in industry as a most important source of technical information.

D. FORMULATION OF THE PROBLEM

(a) The objective problem *vis-à-vis* the closest prior art: reformulation of the problem

11–07   An invention which is the subject of a European patent application is often described and claimed having regard to prior art known to the inventor at the time that the invention was made. In the course of examination or opposition proceedings, further more relevant prior art commonly becomes known, with the result that the problem which the inventor considers himmself to have solved is not the same as the objective problem defined by following the problem-and-solution approach, and in particular, by comparing the technical result of the invention with that achieved by the closest prior art. In such circumstances subjective evidence as to the problems which faced the inventor and the history of the making of the invention may be disregarded,[5] and reformulation of the problem may become necessary.[6]

Such a reformulation should not contradict earlier statements in the application about the general purpose and character of the invention.[7]

---

[3] T254/86 O.J. EPO 1989, 115.
[4] T1/81 O.J. EPO 1981, 439.
[5] *e.g.* T24/81 O.J. EPO 1983, 133.
[6] *e.g.* T1/80 O.J. EPO 1981, 206; T184/82 O.J. EPO 1984, 261; T13/84 O.J. EPO 1986, 253.
[7] T155/85 O.J. EPO 1988, 87.

(b) Avoiding hindsight: proper definition of the problem

Knowledge of the claimed invention must not be taken into account **11–08** when assessing inventive step. Examination with regard to inventive step is limited to the question of obviousness in the overall light of the state of the art and from the viewpoint of the closest prior art (looking forward) and not from that of the invention (looking backward).[8]

In accordance with the problem-and-solution approach, knowledge of the claimed invention and its effect is necessarily used both when determining what is the closest prior art and when defining the problem to be solved by the skilled person *vis-à-vis* such closest prior art. The avoidance of hindsight when following the problem-and-solution approach depends primarily upon an objective definition of the problem to be solved.

The importance of a fair approach to the definition of the objective problem to be solved, following comparison between the effect of the closest prior art and that of the claimed invention, has been frequently emphasised.[9]

E. Assessment of Inventive Step

Having established the objective problem to be solved *vis-à-vis* the closest prior art, the question whether or not the claimed invention was obvious to a "person skilled in the art" has to be considered in every case.

(a) Technical considerations

(i) Nature of the skilled person

The practical orientation of a skilled person wiithin the meaning of **11–09** Article 56 EPC should be emphasised. The teaching of a document may have narrower implications for a person skilled in the art and broader implications for a potential inventor who first recognises the problem on which his future invention is to be based. The assessment of inventive step must consider solely the limited teaching for the person skilled in the art.[10]

It may be appropriate in some cases to consider the problem with the specialised knowledge of a person skilled in a different art from that which forms the subject matter of the claimed invention. If the problem prompts the person skilled in the art to seek its solution in another technical field, the specialist in that field is the person qualified to solve the problem. The assessment of whether the solution involves an inventive step must therefore be based on that specialist's knowledge and ability.[11]

---

[8] T181/82 O.J. EPO 1984, 401.
[9] *e.g.* T5/81 O.J. EPO 1982, 249; T229/85 O.J. EPO 1987, 237; T99/85 O.J. EPO 1987, 413.
[10] T5/81 O.J. EPO 1982, 249.
[11] T32/81 O.J. EPO 1982, 225.

In some cases the notional skilled person is regarded as a team of appropriate specialists.

(ii) Common general knowledge

11–10　A person skilled in the art carries within him the common general knowledge of the particular art in which he is skilled. As to what constitutes such common general knowledge, see also paragraphs 6–10 *et seq.*, since the same level of knowledge is applicable when considering the questions of sufficient disclosure and inventive step.[12] Clearly, handbooks and textbooks (in any language[13]) are generally recognised as forming part of the common general knowledge.

In many technical fields, the common general knowledge is not available in written form, *e.g.* textbooks. In such cases, the extent of common general knowledge has to be assessed on the basis of the available evidence.

The basic principles which form part of the common general knowledge in a particular situation will frequently be known to the parties and the EPO without specific proof. In appropriate cases, however, substantiation as to what constitutes common general knowledge may be necessary.

(iii) The technical features to be considered

11–11　In the absence of any indication to the contrary in the wording of a claim, it must be assumed, when examining for inventive step, that the claim is directed solely to the simultaneous application of all its features.[14]

Nevertheless, in assessing the inventive step of a combination of features, consideration must be given to a feature only if the applicant has provided evidence that it contributes, either independently or in conjunction with one or more of the other features, to the solution of the problem set in the description.[15] Thus, the inclusion in a claim of features which do not contribute to the solution of the objective problem to be solved cannot make a claimed invention inventive if it is otherwise obvious. Similarly, if the applicant acknowledges that certain claimed features were not intended to provide an inventive step, these features and any advantages resulting therefrom can be disregarded in assessing the inventive step, and investigation as to non-obviousness can be confined to the remaining features of the claim.[16]

(iv) Combination of teachings

11–12　In the majority of cases before the EPO in which a finding of lack of inventive step is made, the finding is based upon a combination of teachings from documents.

---

[12] T60/89 O.J. EPO 1992, 268.
[13] T426/88 O.J. EPO 1992, 427.
[14] *Ibid.*
[15] T175/84 O.J. EPO 1989, 71.
[16] T37/82 O.J. EPO 1984, 71; T22/81 O.J. EPO 1983, 226.

A combination of teachings from different prior art documents or sources, including the "closest prior art," may result in finding a lack of inventive step, if such a combination was obvious to a skilled person at the filing date. It is normally regarded as part of the skill of a skilled person that, being aware of the literature in his own and related fields, he is in principle capable of seeking and recognising technical developments which can be derived from simple combinations of documents within such literature.[17]

All previously published embodiments which offered a suggestion to the skilled practitioner for solving the problem addressed must be taken into consideration, even where those embodiments were not particularly emphasised.[18]

When a feature, which is lacking from the closest prior art document, is known from a second document in the same specialised field, and solves the relevant problem, then the fact that the skilled person would not encounter difficulties in applying this known feature to the disclosure of the closest prior art document demonstrates that the documents are not conflicting and that an inventive step is lacking.[19]

It is considered as forming part of the normal activities of the person skilled in the art to select from the prior art materials which are known to him as suitable for a certain purpose the most appropriate one, even in a case where he is presented with only an unreasoned preference for a specific material in the closest prior art document art.[20]

If a skilled person who operates apparatus according to a prior document would undoubtedly discover certain deficiencies in a part of it, and does not possess the technical knowledge to overcom such deficiencies, he can be expected to consult the relevant prior art for components which perform the same function and are better able to meet the requirements.[21]

(v) Unforeseeable or unsuggested results

Unforeseeable advantageous results achieved from a combination of **11–13** known features may indicate the presence of inventive step.[22]

(vi) No pointer: feature disclosed for a different purpose

The use of a known feature for a different purpose than that described **11–14** in the closest prior art document may involve an inventive step, since the relevant disclosure gives no pointer to the claimed solution of the objective problem.[23]

---

[17] *e.g.* T24/81 O.J. EPO 1983, 133.
[18] *Ibid.*
[19] T142/84 O.J. EPO 1987, 112.
[20] T21/81 O.J. EPO 1983, 15.
[21] T15/81 O.J. EPO 1982, 2.
[22] *e.g.* T2/81 O.J. EPO 1982, 394; T39/82 O.J. EPO 1982, 419.
[23] T4/83 O.J. EPO 1983, 498.

(vii) Need for a series of steps

11–15   If, in order to proceed from the known art to the invention a series of steps are necessary, this may be considered as a significant indicator of the presence of inventiveness, particularly in a case where the last decisive step is not known from the prior art and is not derivable therefrom, although such step may at first sight seem to be a very simple one.[24]

(viii) Neighbouring versus remote fields of technology

11–16   The relevant state of the art to be assessed is not limited to that with which the claimed invention is directly concerned.

It is normally regarded as part of the skill of the skilled person that when confronted with a problem he will consider relevant developments within fields of technology which are adjacent to his own (sometimes after enlisting the help of a specialist in such a neighbouring field). The state of the art to be considered therefore includes, as well as that in the specific field of the application, the state of any relevant art in neighbouring fields and/or a broader general field of which the specific field is a part, that is to say any field in which the same problem of one similar to it arises and of which the person skilled in the art of the specific field must be expected to be aware.

What is a neighbouring field is a question of fact, and depends on whether the person skilled in the art seeking a solution to a given problem would take into account developments in such a neighbouring field.[25]

Solutions of general technical problems in non-specific (general) fields must be considered to form part of the general technical knowledge which *a priori* is to be attributed to those skilled persons versed in any specific technical field.[26]

(ix) Unexpected technical progress

11–17   A number of decisions have relied upon unexpected progress compared to the closest prior art as a sufficient indication of inventive step.[27]

Even small improvements may imply the presence of inventive step.[28]

On the other hand, if the claimed invention provides technical progress in comparison with the closest prior art, but such progress would be expected to be achieved in the light of the objective problem to be considered, such progress does not support inventive step.[29]

The use of a known material, on the basis of its known properties, to obtain a known effect, is not normally inventive (being an "analogous substitution"), in the absence of special circumstances.[30]

---

[24] T113/82 O.J. EPO 1984, 10.
[25] T176/84 O.J. EPO 1986, 50.
[26] T195/84 O.J. EPO 1986, 121.
[27] *e.g.* T22/82 O.J. EPO 1982, 341.
[28] *e.g.* T38/84 O.J. EPO 1984, 368.
[29] *e.g.* T24/81 O.J. EPO 1983, 133; T192/82 O.J. EPO 1984, 415.
[30] T130/89 O.J. EPO 1991, 514.

It is sometimes necessary to balance a surprising advantage against concurrent disadvantages.[31]

Furthermore, in some cases it may be necessary to assess the overall effect of tests under varying conditions.[32]

(x) Comparative tests

In some cases the surprising results achieved by the claimed invention **11–18** can be shown by means of comparative tests: unexpected technical progress has to be demonstrated in comparison with the closest prior art, and not merely with the closest marketed prior art.[33]

Where comparative tests are chosen to demonstrate an inventive step with an improved effect over a claimed area, the nature of the comparison with the closest state of the art must be such that the effect is convincingly shown to have its origin in the distinguishing feature of the invention. For this purpose it may be necessary to modify the elements of comparison so that they differ only by such a distinguishing feature.[34]

(xi) Technical progress

Technical progress is not a requirement for inventiveness and paten- **11–19** tability under the EPC. Nevertheless, lack of technical progress may well indicate a lack of inventive step.[35]

In particular, there is no invention in merely making the prior art worse, especially if such consequence is substantially foreseeable, even if some aspect of the results may not be accurately predictable.[36]

(xii) Additional unexpected (bonus) effects

It sometimes happens that a claimed invention not only shows improved **11–20** properties that would be expected, but also an additional, unexpected property or advantage. If the improved but expected properties would be part of routine development by a skilled person, the claimed invention may be regarded as obvious on this basis and therefore effectively in the public domain, regardless of the fact that an extra effect (possibly unforeseen) is obtained.[37] This is particularly the case where a lack of alternatives leads to a "one-way-street" situation, leading to both predictable advantages and a bonus effect.

The presence of unexpected properties for a claimed invention must be balanced against the freedom of a skilled person to use that which is already obvious from the state of the art.

---

[31] T254/86 O.J. EPO 1989, 115.
[32] T57/84 O.J. EPO 1987, 53.
[33] T181/82 O.J. EPO 1984, 401; T164/83 O.J. EPO 1987, 149.
[34] T197/86 O.J. EPO 1989, 371.
[35] T22/82 O.J. EPO 1982, 341; T119/82 O.J. EPO 1984, 217.
[36] T155/85 O.J. EPO 1988, 87.
[37] T21/81 O.J. EPO 1983, 15; T192/82 O.J. EPO 1984, 415.

(xiii) "Could" versus "would"

11–21   The question of inventive step is often decided having regard to whether a skilled person would have arrived at the claimed solution to a problem (as compared to whether he could have done so). In other words, the assessment of inventive step has depended upon the extent to which a skilled person would have been technically motivated towards the claimed invention.[38]

(xiv) Simplification

11–22   When a claimed invention is characterised by its simplicity, there is an inevitable risk that it appears obvious in retrospect. The importance of assessing such inventions without the benefit of hindsight must be emphasised. For example, what at first sight appears to be an obvious step of incorporating a known device in a known machine may not be such if there is evidence that this results in simplification of design coupled with improved performance in use and the solution of a long-standing problem. There is a danger that the difficulty of developing a simple solution without sacrifice of quality will be disregarded when obviousness is assessed with the benefit of hindsight.[39]

(b) Circumstantial indications

11–23   The applicability of what are sometimes called "secondary indicia" for inventive step (i.e. long-felt want, overcoming a prejudice, commercial success) has been recognized in a number of cases. Nevertheless, as a generality such potential indications of an inventive step are often regarded as secondary compared to the technical considerations discussed in the previous section.

(i) Long-felt want: the time factor

11–24   The fact that the state of the art has been inactive over a long period prior to the invention may be an indication that an inventive step is involved if during that time an urgent need for improvement has demonstrably existed.[40]

Normally such a "time factor" in a field of technical interest and commercial importance is used as corroboration of a finding of inventive step which as already been deduced on the basis of other reasoning.

(ii) Overcoming a prejudice

11–25   The existence of a prejudice in the art may be an indication that an inventive step was required in order to overcome it.[41] However, those who wish to rely on a prejudice which might have diverted the skilled man

---

[38] T2/83 O.J. EPO 1984, 265; T265/84 [1987] EPOR 193.
[39] T106/84 O.J. EPO 1985, 132; see also T229/85 O.J. EPO 1987, 237; T9/86 O.J. EPO 1988, 12.
[40] T109/82 O.J. EPO 1984, 473; T271/84 O.J. EPO 1987, 405.
[41] T18/81 O.J. EPO 1985, 166.

away from the invention have the onus of demonstrating the existence of such prejudice.[42]

(iii) Commercial success

In some cases, evidence of commercial success may play a major role in **11–26** the assessment of inventive step if it can be shown that this success derives from the claimed invention.[43] Occasionally, commercial success has been relied on as an additional indication supporting a finding of inventive step.[44]

(c) Special cases

(i) Perceiving the problem

The discovery of an unrecognised problem may in certain circumstances **11–27** give rise to patentable subject matter in spite of the fact that the claimed solution is retrospectively trivial and in itself obvious.[45]

This kind of invention is outside the mechanism of the problem-and-solution approach to the assessment of inventive step, since the problem cannot be identified without hindsight.

On the other hand, the posing of a new problem does not represent a contribution to the inventive merits of the solution if it could have been posed by the average person skilled in the art. Such is the case where a problem consists solely of eliminating deficiencies in an object which comes to light when it is in use.[46]

Problems which are no more than obvious desiderata in a given situation cannot contribute to inventiveness.[47]

(ii) Analogy processes

Chemical products are sometimes protected by claims to an "analogy **11–28** process", *i.e.* defining a known process for producing the new product.

The character of the product, including its novelty and obviousness in the light of the state of the art, has a decisive role in the assessment of the inventive step, because the effect of the process manifests itself in the result, *i.e.* in the product.[48]

The reverse is also true: an analogy process leading to a known or obvious product is normally regarded as not inventive.

(iii) Chemical intermediates

Different views have been expressed as to the factors to be taken into **11–29** account when assessing the inventiveness of a novel intermediate product.

---

[42] T119/82 O.J. EPO 1984, 217.
[43] T191/82 O.J. EPO 1985, 189.
[44] T106/84 O.J. EPO 1985, 132.
[45] T2/83 O.J. EPO 1984, 265.
[46] T109/82 O.J. EPO 1984, 473.
[47] T15/81 O.J. EPO 1982, 2; T195/84 O.J. EPO 1986, 121.
[48] T119/82 O.J. EPO 1984, 217.

In one case, a novel intermediate product was claimed in conjunction with claims to a process for preparing an end product. The process was held to involve an inventive step. The intermediate was also held to involve an inventive step on the basis that it opened the way to the new and inventive chemical process for preparing the known and desired end product.[49]

In another case, a novel intermediate was claimed in the context of a non-inventive "analogy process" for preparing an end product. In this circumstance it was held that such an intermediate could only be considered to involve an inventive step if the intermediate provided a structural contribution to the end product. Even then, the inventiveness of the intermediate had to be assessed in the light of the state of the art.[50]

Following this approach, in a further case it was held that the superior effect of subsequent products which are neither novel nor inventive is not sufficient to render the intermediate inventive.[51]

In a subsequent case it was held that a new chemical intermediate product is not inventive merely because it is prepared in the course of an inventive multi-stage process and is further processed to a known end product.[52]

In a more recent case,[53] however, this approach was not followed. It was held that the same criteria which are generally decisive for determining whether the preparation of a new chemical substance is to be regarded as inventive should in principle also be applied when the substance in question is an intermediate. The sole determing factor is whether or not its preparation enhances the art in a non-obvious way. An intermediate intended for the preparation of a known end product is deemed to be inventive if its preparation takes place in connection with inventive preparation or inventive further processing, or in the course of an inventive complete process.

Further development of the jurisprudence in this area can be expected.

---

[49] T22/82 O.J. EPO 1982, 341.
[50] T65/82 O.J. EPO 1983, 327.
[51] T18/88 O.J. EPO 1992, 107.
[52] T163/84 O.J. EPO 1987, 301.
[53] T648/88 O.J. EPO 1991, 292.

Index